UNLIMITED OPTIONS

UNLIMITED OPTIONS
How to Solve Your IRS Problems Without Losing Everything

Expert
Press
www.ExpertPress.net

ISBN: 978-1-956220-26-1

Expert Press
2 Shepard Hills Court
Little Rock, AR 72223
www.ExpertPress.net

Editing by Dana De Greff
Copyediting by Lori Price
Proofreading by Heather Dubnick
Text design and composition by Emily Fritz
Cover design by Casey Fritz

UNLIMITED OPTIONS

HOW TO SOLVE YOUR IRS PROBLEMS *WITHOUT* LOSING EVERYTHING

ANTONIO NAVA, EA

TESTIMONIALS

Antonio is a very dedicated Tax Relief Professional who focuses on serving taxpayers in need of tax assistance. His extensive experience allows him to serve his clients with the best resolution options available. He is great to work with.

—Jesus Abikarram, EA

As a tax professional myself, Mr. Antonio Nava has been crucial for my growth, not only for the example he sets, but how he has inspired me to grow. He is undoubtedly supporting the growth of the tax professional community, which is hungry for information. One thing I've learned, as Mr. Nava says, "Knowledge gives us power." We have been able to work together in solving tax resolution cases for my clients, and thanks to Mr. Nava and his team, his wisdom, and his enormous desire to serve and share, I have experienced professional growth. I am immensely grateful to him and hope the successes and blessings continue in his career and life.

—Gladiola Unzueta, Financial Coach

I've known Mr. Nava for over ten years and have personally seen his development as a professional and a leader. His knowledge of the tax code combined with his unique perspective as an immigrant entrepreneur makes him a great asset in any negotiation or boardroom. His ability to decipher complex tax law and explain it in layman's terms has led to a loyal following of tax professionals who admire and respect him. I look forward to many more years of business seminars and social gatherings with Mr. Nava.

—Antonio Martinez EA, Founder of NEGOZEE

I am an admirer of Mr. Antonio Nava, who has inspired not only me, but all the members of the tax preparation industry to be a professional in the tax area—to reach a superior level—to feel that our gaze must be on the vision, on the projection, and on the future with responsibility. Mr. Antonio not only maintains a contagiously positive energy, but also manages a leadership model worthy of imitation, leads us to improve our practice as tax professionals, and, best of all, facilitates our practice with the case resolution model before the IRS. Mr. Antonio is a role model as a professional, an immigrant, a human being, a leader of his own life, a leader in the industry, and an example of how far we can go. I am very grateful to Mr. Nava for all he has given us, how he inspires us to thrive, and for the moments of meeting and learning that have been an honor. Thank you for taking us to another level.

—Claudia Saenz, Enrolled Agent and CEO of Tax Solutions & Bookkeeping, Business Coach and Mentor.

Meeting Mr. Nava has been one of the most rewarding experiences of my life. With his expertise, I've evolved as a certified tax preparer, and he's also taught me how to run my office. One of the more effective methods I recall is his focus on turning our profession into a business. I'm still learning, thanks to his help as an instructor and the ease with which he describes his experience in the industry and his ability to offer services. Thank you, Mr. Nava!

—Liliana Mendez, EA, IRS Tax Specialist, CAA

I had the honor of meeting Mr. Antonio Nava in 2018 at a tax event. His way of teaching and giving value to our work caught my attention. At the end of 2018, I invited him to come lead a seminar in San José, California, which he *decided to call "Take Your Practice to Another Level," which was a complete success; we all left shocked by everything we had learned. The same students immediately began asking for another seminar, so Mr. Nava had to return to San José in October 2019 to hold another corporate seminar, which was also a success. It has been a blessing to attend Mr. Nava's classes because not only does he teach the theoretical part, but he also shows us cases of real-life scenarios, and this is very valuable for us. He doesn't just hand us a book and tell us to read it; instead, he encourages us to take our practice to the next level. I am currently collaborating with him under his "Tax Resolution" program to help my clients who come to my office with tax and audit problems. Thanks to this program, my clients have been able to resolve their cases successfully, and they have saved a lot of money. My professional life took a 365-degree turn since I met Mr. Nava, and I have learned to give value to my services. I'd like to express my gratitude to him directly for always giving me advice, accepting my calls regarding tax issues, and never leaving me to fend for myself. I am thankful for him for allowing me to collaborate in assisting more clients with tax problems, and for my profession to advance. I have nothing but admiration for him, his family, and his coworkers.*

—Mayra L. Rodriguez

CONTENTS

INTRODUCTION

This book is dedicated to anyone who feels like they can't find a way out, or perhaps believe there are no alternatives to a difficult situation. What I have learned in my life, over and over again, is there will always be options. The important thing is to look for them—if you're open, they will appear at the right and most convenient moment for you. Opportunities, however, do not usually knock on our doors, and therefore many times they go completely ignored. As you read this book, I invite you to be alert and open to opportunities today, tomorrow, and beyond. In this book we will discuss and explore the options available to you to solve your IRS problems without losing everything.

CHAPTER ONE

MY STORY AND HOW I GOT HERE

I was born in a very small town in Mexico called Chalchihuites, located in the state of Zacatecas. I grew up there in a family of very modest means as the eldest of seven children. Everybody, including my grandparents on both sides, were small business owners, and my father had a small market where he always worked. I had a quiet and happy childhood, but then my life totally changed on Friday, May 16, 1975. This was soon after spending a week with my parents on my first vacation with them, a trip to the city of Guadalajara. I remember we left on a Sunday and came back on Thursday, May 15. The next day my father, as he did every week, went to the city of Durango to buy merchandise, like fruits and vegetables, for the market.

He usually left early, around five in the morning, and that day was no different. A little bit later in the morning, I was in the kitchen having breakfast with my mom when someone knocked on the door and said that my father, along with four people who were traveling in a pickup truck with him, had been involved in an accident and died. This was a huge shock, because at the age of fifteen, not only did I lose my father, but I also became the man of the house. I remember my mother crying loudly but I didn't say anything; I didn't understand how he could have been there in the morning saying goodbye to us, and then suddenly, he was gone.

That day, and many days afterward, were very painful and difficult for me and my family, and I didn't see many options for us in our situation. I was the eldest son, and I felt like I had to take care of everything, despite being a child myself. Not only had we lost my father, but the money he was carrying from the market was gone too. We had no money, and Chalchihuites didn't provide many employment opportunities, not to mention my mother had never worked outside of the home. People came to our house to offer condolences the day of his death, but nobody outside of my grandparents offered real support; they just kept asking us how we were going to survive without my father.

I learned something important that day and in the days soon after—I learned I couldn't sit and wallow or do nothing, and I told myself that I was going to take care of my mom and siblings, no matter what it took. Soon after, I started doing the same thing my father used to do every week—going either Thursday or Friday from Chalchihuites to the city of Durango to buy merchandise, then coming back to sell it in the marketplace on the weekends, using the money to support my family.

While I was working, I was also studying in Durango from Monday to Thursday. That lasted for a couple of years, from around May 1975 to October 1977. I was studying to be an engineer, but when my father passed, I decided to switch and study accounting instead. For a long time, I wasn't happy with anything or anybody, including God. I was mourning the loss of my father, not understanding why I had to be the breadwinner and deal with all these new pressures. But then, things started to shift when I began to feel the satisfaction of being able to help my mother and my six siblings. To be honest, I felt very proud of myself and started to trust in God again, to embrace everything that happened and everything I didn't have control of. Even when we think we have everything against us, we have options.

In terms of the market, we started to lose clientele; it was very hard for me to pay attention in school, so eventually I stopped going to class. One day, a couple of friends of mine decided they were going to go to the United States to look for work; I went with them, crossing the border without any documents nor any real plan. In the eighties, though, it was easy to find a job. I worked, saved money, and sent most of it back home to support my family. I lived in Southern California, very close to the beach, in a house with a bunch of other young kids and people from my hometown—we were all working and having fun. I stayed and worked there for a couple of years until my mother asked me to come back to Mexico.

Fast forward a bit—I got married in 1985 and we had our first baby in 1986. We decided it would be better to live and work in the United States, so I moved back to California on July 4, 1986, with plans to bring my wife and child once I got things established. At the time, I didn't understand the language or the culture. I was by myself, living in a garage with someone who very nicely opened the doors to me, and I was focused on finding a job. The language barrier got in the way, though, and it wasn't until I met another young man who put in a word for me at a restaurant that I got a job as a dishwasher.

It's no exaggeration when I tell you that after that first day of work, my hands were almost bleeding, and I couldn't feel my back. I had never spent time in the kitchen, because that was what my mom did. But I did it, and worked hard; one day, one of the managers came to me (he later became one of my mentors) and told me that I didn't look like a dishwasher. Then he asked what I used to do in Mexico. I told him, and then he said that while it was fine that I was working there now, I needed to find a way to get out. And I kept those words in my mind.

That conversation motivated me to work harder and live by one of my favorite quotes from author and motivational speaker, Jim Rohn, who said, "Work more than what you get paid for as an investment for your future."

I got to the US on Friday, July 4, 1986; the first question I asked of the person who opened his door to me was where I could start taking English classes, because I told myself I needed to understand the language to advance in life. So now I was working like crazy, plus attending school in the morning for two hours from Monday to Thursday.

After a few months of working as a dishwasher, I asked the manager to give me the opportunity to become a busboy. While he agreed, he told me they couldn't pay me; still, I was clear I just wanted the opportunity. I bussed tables, and then I asked to do the same thing as a bartender. Eventually, I went on to work in every single area of the restaurant, except in the kitchen. Sure, I didn't get paid, but I considered it all to be an investment for my future. And it was, because every time they needed someone to fill in, who do you think they called? After a few years, I was the assistant general manager in charge of the operations of the restaurant with over forty employees. And I started as a dishwasher.

What I'm saying is this: You need to look out for the opportunities in life. When I lost my father, I found the opportunity to somehow continue what he was doing when he was alive. Then I went to the US, and I strived for more than what I had. It doesn't matter what we do. We must always give more than what we get paid. That's my mantra, and it's exactly what I've been doing every single day of my life—providing more value than what I get paid.

One day, a big thing happened. The owner of the restaurant said that he wanted to open a restaurant in the city of Newport Beach, and he wanted me to run it. It was a huge responsibility and opportunity, and I took it. I moved with my family from San Fernando Valley to Costa Mesa, next to Newport Beach, in 1991. I started working there and continued going to school, but this time, it wasn't for English—I was pursuing a certificate in accounting.

Unfortunately, the restaurant didn't stay open, but instead of looking for another job right away, I decided to focus on getting my certificate in accounting in December 1993 and then starting my own business, even though we had only $2,000 in savings. Once I got certified, I started my business from our home, but the problem was I didn't have any clients. So, I got up early in the mornings, and with my oldest daughter who was seven years old, started delivering flyers and business cards, totally confident that I was going make it happen.

Around that same time, my wife got a phone call that led to someone telling me about a man in San Clemente, who had a small practice in accounting. He had very few clients, but I was told he would probably give me some business tips if I asked. I drove to San Clemente and after I talked to him for a bit, he offered to sell me his practice. Apparently, he had another practice closer to home; his drive to San Clemente was more than eighty miles every day. I told him I was interested but

I had no money, which left us at a crossroads. We both wanted to make it work, but it didn't seem like it would.

Soon after, he invited me to lunch with him and another friend. Both of them had a few alcoholic drinks that day, while I only drank water. Everyone went their separate ways and later, I found out that he got a DUI. A couple of days later, he called me and said that he couldn't drive, so he wanted to sell me the practice—and give me about fifty clients—for $5,000. He said I could pay in installments, and so I agreed.

On Friday, December 28, 1993, I got the key and went to the office—my office—and opened the door. The feeling I had when I opened the door of my practice for my clients . . . well, it was amazing! It was the opportunity I had been looking for in my life; it was everything I had been working for. Everything started that day for me, and I haven't looked back since.

CHAPTER TWO

WHY SOME PEOPLE GET INTO TAX PROBLEMS

Before getting too deep into the details of why people find themselves mired in tax problems, it's important to remember that in order to minimize the risk of having a tax or IRS problem, you should adhere to the following steps: First, be in compliance by filing your tax returns before the due date; second, make your estimated tax payments on time; third, if you have people who work for you, make a correct classification of those workers (either as employees or independent contractors); fourth, pay your payroll tax because those late payments and fines can be very, very steep; and lastly, have a reliable system to identify your income and expenses so that you can create some tax planning strategies and minimize your tax liability now and in the future. This may at first seem like a lot, but when you follow all these steps, you'll be surprised at how second nature it will become, and also it will save you stress and perhaps even money in the future. Talk about a win!

It's a good idea to understand and recognize some of the common errors made by employees and employers so that you know what to watch out for if you have a business. And don't worry if you don't know how to properly file a tax form or have questions at all—the IRS has a lot of information on their website at www.irs.gov, or you can hire a professional to help; in the best-case scenario, you'll save time and money in the long run, and in the worst case, you'll avoid punishment by the IRS (both of which are positive outcomes).

To start our discussion about where many problems come from when dealing with taxes, we're going to focus on those who are employees.

The following are some of the most common errors made by employees:

- Not having correct withholding from their paycheck
- Expensive lifestyle
- Claiming tax credits they are not entitled to
- Claiming dependents they are not entitled to
- Not reporting all the income they receive
- The sale of a capital asset
- Cancellation of a debt
- Math errors
- Tax protestors (those who argue that paying taxes is illegal)

A lot of the issues that arise with employees start with withholding, or the amount of money an employer will take from their employees' paychecks and pay to the IRS in their name. If you, as an employee, do not have the correct withholding of tax from your paycheck, you are getting a free ticket for a tax problem; in other words, you are essentially taking money from the government and they don't appreciate that—just like anyone else wouldn't. If you are tempted at all to do this, I would say save yourself the trouble and don't!

To give you an example from my own life, back when I had the practice in San Clemente, I remember there was an expensive restaurant about ten miles from my office. From one day to the next, I started losing clients who were employees of that restaurant because they had miraculously found an expert on tax preparation who specialized in working with those who were waitresses and waiters. This man claimed to be an expert on tax preparation for wage earners; I wanted to mention this here because I have seen many employees get in trouble because they hire people who claim to be "experts" in whatever specific area they work in. In every area of work, people try to claim expenses they're not allowed, just like people try to claim dependents and credits they are not allowed. If something feels too good to be true, if you're getting a lot of money back, or someone is claiming you won't have to pay any taxes or minimum tax to the IRS, my best advice is to run the other way.

Another area I have found that gets people into sticky situations is an expensive lifestyle. It makes sense, in a way, right? The more money you get, the more freedom you have to buy things you couldn't before, and a lot of people start to change their lifestyle, either buying up property or cars, taking expensive vacations, purchasing jewelry and clothes, and other luxury goods. That's all fine and good—we should enjoy this life while we can—but what happens if suddenly, with this new lifestyle, you don't have the money to pay your back taxes? This might not be horrible, but what I see happen far too often is that people will continue as always and end up spending even more money, digging an even bigger hole for themselves instead of trying to correct the behavior.

Sometimes the reasons for which employees get into problems with the IRS have more to do with incorrectly claiming credits they aren't entitled to, and in recent years there have been issues with those claiming tax credits for higher education. With my own practice, there was an uptick in these cases, and I started getting a lot of clients with problems in this area. Naturally, because they were claiming credits in education, I would ask them questions about school, and half the time they would admit they never even went to school. Unfortunately, the IRS doesn't deal in wishful thinking or in what we would like to do, so if you haven't been to school, it doesn't make sense to file for an education credit; if you do, make sure the educational institution is participating in the program before enrolling and making an investment.

Another area that gets people into trouble, and one for which the IRS is on high alert, is claiming dependents they are not entitled to. Potential clients will come into my office saying they want to claim a person, and then—to test them—when I ask if the dependent is their relative or is living with them, they will say, "No, but I have their Social Security number." That is absolutely not legal and will never be excused by the IRS. Sometimes people try to game the system by sharing children, which is also not allowed; in short, if you are claiming dependents who are not complying with the rules, including not being related to you or under your guardianship, you're not allowed to file for this credit.

Of course, errors can be made—both accidentally and on purpose—in math, especially when employees try to prepare their own taxes using programs like Turbo Tax. While it's an intuitive and streamlined process, the problem with these programs is that you control the results, and sometimes people create the results they want to see but aren't necessarily based in reality. It can be tempting to change numbers around in the tax report, to add a zero here or take a zero away there, but that will get you in trouble sooner or later; so, if you do file your own taxes, please remember to be accurate—yes, but also honest.

We also have the tax protestors, those who feel or believe it is somehow illegal to pay taxes in this country.

This is a group which gets in trouble easily because they don't file anything, and sometimes they refuse to do so for years or even decades. The amount of money they end up owing when they're caught can ruin lives; in the end, it's not worth it to pay all those fines and fees out of a sense of justice or principles or whatever it may be. Taxes are what help with infrastructure, pay for our roads and schools, and help care for the sick. If you look at it that way, while losing money may be painful or inconvenient in the short term, in the long term, we need taxes for many of the benefits we enjoy in this country.

And finally, not reporting the sale of a capital asset or the cancellation of a debt may lead to an additional tax on your return.

I hope this chapter has been illuminating and informative. Next, we'll discuss in more detail small business owners, including sole proprietors and business entities like partnerships, LLCs, and corporations. If this applies to you, you'll want to pay close attention, and if it doesn't—well, you never know when it might!

CHAPTER THREE

WHY SOME BUSINESSES GET INTO TAX PROBLEMS

To start, I want to assure you that if you are a small business owner and you have issues with the IRS, you are not alone and there is a way out. If you aren't in trouble, then this next section will help make sure you stay in good standing. From my decades of experience working with small business owners, I've noticed that one of the main reasons they have issues with the IRS is because they don't keep good books and records. When I receive new clients, one of the first things I request is their financial reports, a detailed breakdown of their profits and losses including the total income they received during the year from their business, as well as the expenses calculated. The report is essential because it shows a business's total sales as well as its total expenses, and this is also where trouble often starts.

A lot of times business owners may have a summary of income and expenses, but when you look at them more closely, those numbers don't really add up. Often, it seems like someone was in a rush or making up numbers, which tells me that they don't keep any records at all, or they put them together before meeting with me, or at the last minute right before taxes were due to the IRS. In other words, the report may have been put together simply to meet the responsibility to file the tax return and not to provide an accurate look into the business.

The problem, of course, is that the IRS invests millions of dollars every year to create profiles on taxpayers, especially those who are business owners, and they divide them up by industry, services, profession, and activity. They will then carefully compare the sales specific businesses had in a reported year, and then move on to the expenses they had; when the system receives the tax return the owner submits, and they see for whatever reason something doesn't add up, the tax return will be sent out for examination. And that's when you'll have nowhere to run because at the end of the day, numbers don't lie.

On the other hand, what I tell my clients is if we have an accurate, detailed, and up-to-date monthly profit and loss system set up, we can then see what's happening right away from the total income the business is generating and the total expenses. From there we can also observe and calculate a net profit or loss, not to mention how the business is producing income, and create planning strategies in order to reduce the tax liability for your business. One of the things I suggest, for example, is to provide employee benefits, buy necessary equipment for the business, and buy real estate within many others planning strategies, but first and foremost we need to have the numbers. That's why having a financial report—a very accurate summary of the income and expenses—will provide an opportunity to create a tax plan to set you up for success and a strategy for reducing the tax liability.

Another area creating problems for business owners is not making their estimated tax payments. For example, let's say your business is generating $10,000 in income every month; this means that every three months (estimated tax payments are made quarterly throughout the year) the business owners will have $30,000 in net income they must legally pay taxes on. According to the rule set up by the IRS, the taxes business owners pay to them happens at the same time every year (April 15, June 15, September 15, and January 15).

Now, if you miss a payment, you will have to catch up on the payment you missed, and it will become more than a one-time payment because it is a combination of past payment due and the current payment. What I see happen again and again is that business owners won't have the money because they already spent it on something else, and now they're in a deeper hole. This is the point where people start to get nervous or panic and maybe even create and make up additional expenses they "forgot" to claim to reduce the tax liability. You can avoid all of this by paying on time every quarter and not relying on wishful thinking when it comes to the IRS; believe me, sooner or later, they'll notice if your numbers are not adding up.

If you own a business, then filing for an extension is another area to be careful with. I've seen many clients fall behind on payments, and then they file for an extension and don't pay, or they just let the tax liability grow even more. It's not uncommon for me to receive clients who haven't paid taxes in years, and while it's not impossible to get out of the situation, the longer you wait, the harder it gets. I also work with clients who come to me without any financial statements whatsoever, or they come with just the bank statements. And while the bank statement helps to start to get an accurate picture of income and expenses, it's not everything.

Let's assume, for example, that you work in construction, and you go to Home Depot to buy some supplies for a project, then you use the receipt from the purchase as proof of an expense on your tax form. Well, the question the agent from the IRS is going to have is how to know these purchases you made in Home Depot were for material for the business, as opposed to your own personal use? You need more than the receipt as proof; otherwise, who is to say you weren't building a house for yourself on the government's dime? This is something I recommend: Every time you go to buy items for your business and at the same time you buy something for your personal needs, use two forms of payment. You pay the business expense with a business account (either a credit card, debit card, or check) and your personal items with a personal bank check or credit/debit card. This way you will create a pattern to help you if someday your tax return is selected for examination.

One area that can potentially create issues, and which not everyone thinks about, is not understanding the language. As I mentioned earlier in the book, when I came to the United States, I didn't know any English. Because of that, of course, it makes sense I wouldn't understand my responsibilities as a taxpayer; many people are in the same situation even after having lived here for years. This is especially common in states like California, Texas, and Florida, where there are larger populations of immigrants. Sometimes people just keep running their business without learning the language. The danger here is you'll miss a lot of your responsibilities, not understand the tax laws, and miss deadlines, which will create huge problems for you and your business, not to mention your employees. My recommendation is to hire someone who can provide you with good advice, and if you don't know the language, don't be afraid to ask for help as there are many professionals who speak more than one language and are happy to offer aid, such as myself.

While we touched a bit on the trouble math errors can get business owners into, it's worth going into more detail here before moving on to the next chapter. When I first started working back in the early nineties, computers weren't as popular as they are now, and believe it or not,

I had to prepare all my tax returns by hand. Human beings not being perfect, that created math errors every once in a while, but now almost everything is done via software. Ironically, there are still math errors made all the time with the advent of software, but not because the computer made a mistake—it's because people put incorrect numbers into the system—for example, $5,000 instead of $500—which is a huge difference!

While I know it can be tempting, I would caution all taxpayers not to cheat the system, because eventually it will catch up with you. The IRS takes great pains to monitor taxpayers, especially those who have businesses, as you are responsible for the payments of others as well. There is also the challenge of staying calm and smart when it comes to your cost of living; sometimes a business owner sees money coming in and they start to change their lifestyle, but it's too much too soon. They buy the dream house, the dream car, they take this vacation, go out to that fancy dinner. As business owners, people need to understand and take seriously that some years will be good, but you can't create a lifestyle based only on the good years because there will be bad years as well.

On a final note, I always advise business owners to invest in an accounting system for their business, no matter how small. I'm not saying you must hire the most expensive CPA available, but, at the very least, you do need to dedicate a few hours per week to your books and records, which will ideally be done by an expert. Block some time on your schedule to organize your receipts, total income, and total expenses to have a clear picture so you'll have the opportunity to make better decisions around your business for the future. Whether you decide to invest time or money, your accounting department must be a top priority in your business, alongside paying payroll taxes on time.

With that in mind, we'll move on to what happens if your tax return is selected for an audit, why it happens, and best strategies for moving forward with success. One final note: If at some point you're thinking about not filing your tax return because you don't have the money to pay for the amount you owe, it's not a good idea not to file because the IRS takes those delinquent returns very seriously, and you'll also get a penalty for not filing before the due date. It's always better to file, and look for someone who can assist you in negotiating your tax liability.

CHAPTER FOUR

THE AUDIT OF A TAX RETURN

There are a few recommended steps I'd like to give when it comes to facing a tax audit. If you're in this situation, don't panic, as there's always a means to an end, especially if you're working with a licensed professional. However, before revealing the details, I think it's important to first start with a discussion about why the IRS would audit a tax return in the first place, and to do that, we need to separate individuals and businesses.

When an individual files a tax return, for example, they do so as an employee, as someone who is working for someone else. That, or perhaps they are someone who generates income from investments or rental properties and is receiving income of some kind. It could also be that they have different sources of income as a contract worker; as long as it's not income from a business they have (unless they are self-employed), then they would file as an individual. So, let's say it's time to file a tax return, and they need to report the income they received during the year; most of the time, this will be simple because they are going to get certain document forms from their employer, such as a W-2 form, which is the most common one.

On the other hand, if the person has some investments, then most likely, they'll also receive some type of form from the company taking care of the money. For example, if you own real estate and you have a property management company, you're going to receive some sort of breakdown, like the rent you've received and the expenses you had otherwise. In this case, you're responsible for your own books or records of the rents you collect. When you receive those forms, it's important to verify the accuracy of them and have a conversation with the people who completed them because, at the end of the day, you're the only responsible person. Another important step is to verify you do not have missing forms because sometimes they get lost, causing you to file an incomplete tax return.

If for any reason the taxpayer didn't receive a specific form—perhaps the business or the person who was supposed to send the form didn't send it, they sent it incorrectly, or it got lost in the mail—then the tax return will be prepared incorrectly. When the IRS receives the tax return, they're going to match the income the taxpayer is reporting with the records they have; if there is any difference, then they'll send a letter to you. This letter is known as a CP2000 letter, which means while they got the tax return from you, the information you provided didn't match their records. Once you receive the letter, then the next step would be to agree or disagree with them.

While it may seem obvious, it's very important to read the letter carefully. Some people may not realize this, but identity theft can occur when you least expect it and can wreak havoc on your financials if you're not paying close attention. It's creating a lot of problems everywhere, not only in the US; because of this, I want to make sure I explain in detail what to look out for. Let's say you receive a letter from the IRS saying they received your tax return, but their records show you didn't report all the income you received. The IRS will detail what they have in their records, and you might find you received income from different sources you don't recognize. The lesson here is to not accept everything blindly, even from the IRS—if you know you didn't receive income from certain places, then it's your duty to disagree and contest it, not only to correct the errors, but to make sure you are not the victim of identity theft.

Another reason the IRS might select a tax return for examination outside of numbers not matching is that sometimes people claim incorrect expenses or incorrect amounts on their tax forms. On the other hand, if your employer requires you to have an office at home or to use your personal car for business, then in those cases, you could claim them under the category of employee business expenses. Just remember to note the amounts correctly so if the IRS has a question about a specific expense and your tax return is selected for examination, you can back up your expenses with proof and receipts.

Most of the time bank accounts are also taken into consideration, but what I've found is a lot of taxpayers are very creative. They think if the IRS audits them, they'll ask for the bank account. They don't deposit all the income they receive or just have the minimum amount required in the bank account, so the IRS won't find the rest. I'm sorry to say it doesn't work that way, because you have a lifestyle just like everyone else, and the lifestyle provides a clue to how much your possible total income is. Also keep in mind, the IRS has the right to contact third parties such as your neighbors, relatives, suppliers, and clients. Therefore, let's play the game with the rules that already exist; as Jesus once said, "Give to Caesar what belongs to Caesar."

For most people, it's embarrassing to have the IRS go to your neighbors and start asking questions about your lifestyle, such as where you like to go, how many vacations you take, where your boat is, how many cars you have, and so on. It's not a pleasant experience, to say the least, which is why the best rule of thumb is to be transparent and honest. If for any reason you have messed up, well, now is the best time to clean up your mistakes. And as the title of this book says, you always have options to negotiate your tax liability. If you don't have the money, yes, they will be more limited, but it's also possible to get some of the penalties negotiated under several programs the IRS has in place.

One of these programs is known as the first-time penalty abatement, or reasonable cause. This is pertinent in situations where you don't have well-organized records—not because you didn't want to—but because something happened, such as a fire, a flood, or any sort of disaster causing you to lose your records. Another situation might be that you didn't receive sound advice from an accountant, and it caused you to make a mistake and file your tax return incorrectly. Of course, it's not automatic for the IRS to remove the penalties altogether, but most of the time you can try to negotiate and reduce them.

We'll switch gears a bit here and move away from individuals to think about why the IRS might audit a tax return from a business owner (which includes business entities such as sole proprietorships, LLCs, and partnerships). In my experience, the IRS will most likely have questions regarding specific lines of the tax returns related to income, and other times it's related to expenses, or a combination of both. And why is that? Because as we already know, you declare in your tax return that you make a specific amount of income, and from there the IRS is going compare your income to what your industry typically generates wherever you're located. If you don't do this correctly, then your tax return may be selected for examination.

They'll also compare other businesses like yours producing around the same amount of income and whether or not they have the expenses you claimed. They'll try to match the tax return you're filing with the information they created in which they have invested potentially millions of dollars not to mention time. They compare and match that information and if questions arise, then they'll approach you with questions about specific items; you'll be selected for a tax return examination and get a nasty letter saying you'll need to call them to schedule an appointment. And this is where it gets serious, and believe me, you don't want to ignore their letters nor avoid meeting with them.

Sometimes these appointments with the IRS are in person, but other times they can be done by telephone— it really depends on the situation. In the worst-case scenario, an agent from the IRS will literally come to your business to see how you run things, how things work, who works there, and more. This is the least ideal situation because the revenue officer is going to be in your business and around all your employees and customers, and they will probably assume you are in trouble, which is not a good look and will add an air of unease. People like to talk, and it won't be good for your business to have the IRS agents there in terms of optics, not to mention the stress and anxiety that comes with it.

In terms of what happens during the actual audit of the tax return, we'll focus first on the taxpayer and— when I say taxpayer—I want to clarify this includes a person or a business entity. When you as the taxpayer receive the letter saying your tax return has been selected for examination, the first thing you need to do (and this is also stated in the letter) is contact the person listed in the letter in order to arrange a conference call or an appointment. As I mentioned earlier, this may be done by telephone, or face-to-face in the IRS office, or face-to-face at your place of business. I can't stress enough that you don't want to put this off—call the person right away to schedule the appointment.

A word to the wise: When you make the phone call, more often than not, the IRS officer is going to be extremely friendly and pleasant, tell you the conversation will be very quick, and they just have some questions to ask you. I mention this because many times after people talk to the IRS agent, they'll call me and ask how much I charge to represent them. And I, of course, will do my due diligence and ask them some questions; afterwards the person will say, "The IRS agent I talked to was very friendly and they told me this would be easy, so why should I pay you or someone else to represent me if I can represent myself?" And I get it, believe me; I can see how this would be tempting, but from my many years of experience, the worst mistake you can ever make is to represent yourself. Unless you are well versed in tax code and tax law, it will be a huge mess, and you'll end up losing time and money.

I'm being transparent here because it happens repeatedly, and I want people to be aware of the risks of taking everything at face value when it comes to getting audited by the IRS. Just because someone is nice and friendly doesn't mean the process will be easy nor will it work out in your favor. After you schedule an appointment, then the real work will begin, and you'll start by organizing your receipts. You'll also need to bring your bank statements, or whatever the item is under examination, which will most likely be stated in the original letter you were sent. If the notice says your income is going to be under examination, then you'll need to bring in the bank statements for sure, because they want to see your income. If the income is not an issue, don't be proactive and provide any information the IRS is not asking for—just stick with what the notice says. And if they do ask for something not stated in the letter, my best advice is to say something like, "I'm not prepared with that information because it's not on the notice I received."

To further illustrate the importance of this process, I'm going to share an experience I had that I'll never forget. One day, I was representing a taxpayer in the IRS office, and we could hear the people in the office next to us (the offices aren't really rooms; there are no walls, but just a bunch of desks), and while you can't see the person sitting next to you, you can hear them. The auditor asked the person if they had any more expenses to report that they didn't report in their tax return. And the person said, "Yes, I have more expenses." The question you may be asking, as I did, was why didn't he list those expenses in the first place? The truth is, most taxpayers think the more expenses they have, the less taxes they'll pay or the higher their refund will be. And so, the person went on because he was in a hole now; he told the agent he was making car payments, had expenses for his child who was in college, one child in soccer classes and another in ballet classes.

Then the agent said, "Okay, is that everything?" The taxpayer, who didn't know anything about tax law, said, "Yes, those are the expenses off the top of my head, but there might be more." The agent then said, with the information he was just given, it meant the person had a balance of several thousand dollars to pay. I just remember there was total silence from the taxpayer, who was probably thinking, *If I have all those expenses, why do I have to pay more taxes?* But the agent knew what the taxpayer was thinking, and right away, before the taxpayer had the opportunity to speak, the agent said, "I was reviewing your tax return, and with the income you reported, there's no way you can pay those expenses. So, I'm assuming you had more income than what's listed on your tax return; you have this tax liability because you didn't pay taxes on all the income you received."

I'll never forget that moment, because it's a perfect example of why you shouldn't represent yourself—that person had no idea what he was getting himself into, and then he ended up leaving with more money owed, more stress, and a feeling of panic. And what usually happens after this moment of reality is the client will come to me, or someone like me, to help them clean up the mess they created. I say all of this to help you avoid problems and unnecessary stress, and, of course, to save you time and money. At the end of the day, it's usually not worth representing yourself unless you are well versed in tax law, which the majority of the population is not. Going back to the previous example, when the auditor asked the taxpayer if he had more expenses to claim, he was really asking for business expenses, which someone with experience in representation would have understood.

Outside of the IRS agent, there are other people you should be aware you may have to deal with when it comes to being audited. To start, the IRS may send you a tax compliance officer, who usually performs the examination of the tax return in their office—though with the pandemic, this was more likely to be performed over the telephone. The other person you may work with is a revenue agent, but this is more common with tax returns related to businesses. When revenue agents go to a business, they will want to see how the business is being run and to avoid any surprises; for example, if the business is reporting $1 million dollars in revenue, but they are really producing several millions of dollars—that will be discovered soon enough. The revenue agent is basically the person who will be working in the field.

At the end of the day, the best-case scenario is not to have the audit happen at your place of business. In my opinion and as a representative of the taxpayer, it's a good way of protecting the taxpayer's rights. While the business is being audited, we try to have the examination done outside of the business's premises, and it's much better to do it that way, in my experience. If it's not possible, then I will ask the examiner to meet with me in the business at a specific time and then tell the business owner to take a break with their employees while I deal with the examiner alone.

These precautions are taken not because we have something to hide, by the way; it's just because it is in the best interest of my client, which is my number one concern. The risk is that sometimes employees talk about different things that can have a negative consequence on the client without them even meaning to or realizing what they are doing, and it's not appropriate to do this while the agent from the IRS is doing the examination or walk-through of the business. As I mentioned earlier, this is not because the taxpayer or business has something to hide, it's simply because—as I demonstrated earlier—a taxpayer can get in trouble by themselves, just by saying things they are not being asked about, or they can be very proactive and start giving information they shouldn't.

Remember, too, when the taxpayer receives the report from the agent, they can agree or disagree with what is in the report. Of course, if they agree, well, then it's a simple matter of signing the report and giving it back to the agent. The agent will then close the file and submit the report to the IRS to make the assessment. Every once in a while, though not very often, the taxpayer will actually receive a refund because the tax return was incorrectly prepared, but it's unlikely, at least from what I have seen in my twenty-nine years of experience. I've never represented someone who received a refund, not because I'm not good at representing clients, but because it's very rare.

And it makes sense, when you think about it. Can you imagine the IRS investing so much in resources and time, doing all of these examinations for tax returns, all to issue a refund instead of collecting money? Doubtful, because it's not in their best business practice to do so. Now, if you do agree with the report, then all you need to do is sign it and send it back to the agent. And the case will later close. In a few weeks or a couple months, you'll receive a letter from the IRS saying they accepted the examination report, but it won't be done just yet. Their supervisor must review what he or she did, approve it, and then the case will be closed. At that point, you'll receive a notice letting you know what amount you owe and the specific time to pay the amount.

But what about if you don't agree with the report or the result of the examination? In that case, when you receive the report, you'll make it known that you disagree by calling the manager of the agent who did the examination and having a conversation with them, which hopefully will result in an agreement on the items you don't agree with. Perhaps you're wondering, though, what happens if you have the conversation with the manager and still don't come to an agreement? The first thing I'd recommend is not to continue with the disagreement, especially if you don't have any basis to prove you're correct; if you're wrong, you're simply going to extend the time and interest accrued, and your penalties are going to be higher, so it's not in your best interest to do that.

Let's say you have a conversation with the manager, and you don't come to an agreement; if you can back up your claims, then you have the right by law to appeal and to submit a disagreement to the appeals department. The appeals department is part of the IRS, but it's also independent, so they will review the case without any favoritism or conflict of interest. As a matter of fact, sometimes the agent who does the examination is very linear. They say, "Okay, in order to accept this item and expense, I want to see these receipts." If for any reason you don't have those receipts, you may lose the right to claim the expense. Sometimes it happens in an examination, but in appeals it's a little different because they listen to you and will often work with you on businesses statistics. On the other hand, working with business statistics is something not usually accepted in examination.

To reiterate, you don't have to agree with the appeals officer. You'll have another opportunity to state your case; if you do disagree, then you'll receive a notice of deficiency. And I always say the notice of deficiency is the key to paradise, because it's basically your last opportunity to appeal the decision. At the same time, it provides you with a huge opportunity because when you receive it, you'll be granted ninety days to submit a petition with the US Tax Court to bring this case to the court.

In my twenty-nine years of experience, I have assisted dozens of taxpayers to open a petition (per se) where they represent themselves before the US Tax

Court. While I'm not an attorney and can't represent a taxpayer before the judge in the US Tax Court, I can do all the administrative work as a representative of the taxpayer, including having a conversation with the chief counsel; once the Tax Court receives the petition, the Court will then notify the IRS to let them know someone is in disagreement and has filed a petition. At this point, the IRS will contact the taxpayer to have a conversation and try to be in an agreement so the case can be closed without going to trial; if that does not happen, then it is sent back to court for trial.

Representatives from the IRS, such as an appeals officer or settlement officer, will try to negotiate the result to avoid a trial. And that's huge, because you can then have a conversation. Both the IRS and the chief council (the authority from the IRS) want to avoid going to trial, at least for the most part. The IRS takes into consideration what we call the hazard of litigation, which is a percentage the IRS has to lose in a case or to give some percentage of the expenses or items the taxpayer claims to disagrees with, which means this conversation is really a negotiation and a lot of times everybody wins. The IRS wins because it can close a case and doesn't have to go through a trial. The Tax Court wins because they have one case not in the booth for trial, and the taxpayer also wins because the longer the case, the more the expenses for representation.

If, for any reason, you're experiencing or might experience a disagreement in an examination from the

IRS, keep these steps in mind because you don't want to lose the opportunity to request a petition with the US Tax Court. Most of the time, you'll get some benefit if you file a petition and have some reasonable basis for what the IRS believes the judge will give you.

In closing, if your tax return has been selected for examination and you don't have very well-organized books and records, such as a summary of the income and the expenses you have, you'll be in a stressful situation. If you don't have an accounting system, or a bookkeeping system, then you really don't have anything to work with. It will be incomplete, and then somehow, you'll need to make a reconstruction of those books by looking at your agenda, the appointments you had, your suppliers, how much you bought in material, etc. My best recommendation is to invest in a good accounting system because if you hire a competent accountant, most of the time you'll have very well-organized books and records. And the best part is, with excellent tax planning, the accountant will get paid with the taxes he or she helped you save.

CHAPTER FIVE

HOW TO WIN AN AUDIT ON EARNED INCOME TAX CREDIT AND CHILD TAX CREDIT

Many people get nervous when they find out they are going to get audited, which is perfectly normal. Most of us already have complicated feelings when it comes to the IRS; movies and televisions shows haven't helped its image much, not to mention sensational news stories about celebrities going to jail for not paying their taxes. The good news is, if you are being audited or if it happens to you at some point, it's not the end of the world; there are plenty of options for you. First, we'll be discussing how best to win an audit, which is an area I am quite familiar with—in fact, I have a special training I provide to tax preparers and people in general who need it or are interested in this topic, not only because I get a lot of satisfaction out of protecting taxpayers' rights, but also because I'm passionate about what I do.

We'll start by focusing on how to win an audit on the Earned Income Tax Credit (EITC), which is a credit for middle- and low-income families that reduces tax liability and, at some point, becomes refundable. For example, let's say your tax liability is $1,000 and you're preparing your tax return, which includes the EITC. After calculating your tax, which we'll say is $1,000, you might have access to credits because you have dependents who allow you to qualify for this type of refundable credit, which could mean an amount of $5,000.

What this does is offset your tax liability (in this case your tax liability is $1,000 and your credit is $5,000), then what usually happens is you'll get $4,000 as a refund on your tax return, which is a huge refund for most people. Because the credit is a significant amount of money, there is, unfortunately, a lot of fraud involved in this area of tax, which means the IRS is aware and vigilant about those who claim these types of credit. Most of the time, this sort of fraud occurs amongst middle- and low-income families because the EITC is supposed to help those with less means. As a result of an excess amount of fraud, the IRS estimates they give away millions of dollars every year to taxpayers who claim these credits but shouldn't, because they don't meet the requirements to qualify.

Now, if you do have dependents and are planning on claiming these credits, you will want to read and pay close attention to Publications 596 and 972 (publications from the IRS with all the requirements and specific details for who qualifies to claim these credits). By reading through these publications, you'll be in a much better position to avoid making any mistakes. The first thing, of course, allowing you to qualify for this type of credit is you must have children, and those children must be claimed on the tax return. Now, if you meet all the requirements, and you are entitled to claim those credits, the next step would be to file a tax return and receive your refund. However, you may not receive the refund, but instead a letter stating there are questions about your dependents. To qualify for your tax credit, you'll need to provide a specific document, or you might receive the refund you're claiming on your tax return, followed by the letter asking for information and documentation.

If this is the case, you'll need to provide paperwork to the IRS—documents and proof you do, in fact, act as the parent or guardian of the children you are claiming and meet all the requirements for the specific credit you are claiming. On that note, I want to give an example related to all of this which happened during a case I had years ago. While I've been working and representing taxpayers for many years, this case in particular sticks out in my mind. I want to share the details here with you so you can have a clear idea of how to win this sort of case and how audits on these credits work.

Having worked in this area for over three decades, I remember one client in particular—a young, single mother with three children. She was in her twenties when she filed a tax return, and the three children she had were very young, one of them only months old. Perhaps one of the reasons she sticks out in my mind is because she worked as a dishwasher in a restaurant, and I did the same thing when I first came to this country to start a new life. I could relate to her and knew how hard that sort of work could be, not to mention trying to support a family on such an income. On top of that, she only worked part-time because she needed to take care of the children when they weren't in school or day care. The total income she made during the year she filed for was around $18,000; just try and imagine making $18,000 a year while living in the United States—in Orange County, no less—one of the most expensive counties in the country. Not a great situation for anyone, let alone a single mother.

The reason she came to me was because after she filed her tax return, the IRS sent her a letter stating they had questions they wanted to clarify; in order to send her a refund, she needed to send them proof of the relationships and all other requirements for the dependents she was claiming to receive the EITC and Child Tax Credit (CTC). Because she was claiming three dependents, the IRS said they needed proof of these relationships— basically, she needed to prove these children lived with her and she met all the other requirements to get the tax credits. The IRS requested documents from my client to prove she was, in fact, the mother of the children, which was overwhelming and not as simple as you might think.

As I mentioned, my client lived in Orange County, California, where the cost of living is quite high, and of course, with $18,000, she didn't have enough money to rent an apartment for herself and her children. It's very common in these situations for several people to share a living space, renting an apartment where one family lives in one bedroom and another family lives in another bedroom or in the garage, for example. This was the situation my client was in—she and her three children rented a small room in an apartment with other people who were not their family. Because of that, she didn't have any utility bills in her name nor a rental agreement. She didn't have anything to prove where she lived nor where her children lived, creating problems for her because the IRS likes to see a paper trail and proof of everything being claimed, especially in an area so rife with fraud.

It also didn't help that she was moving around a lot at the time, which is quite common for those who are living with others or don't have formal rental agreements—sometimes situations change, people move, or need more space or less space, and then they look for a more suitable living situation. They tend to live for a few months in one place, then a few in another, renting one bedroom, and then moving somewhere else that is more affordable or appropriate. Or sometimes it could be they're not happy living with so many people, or they don't like the neighborhood and they decide to move again. Because of this, it's common for these taxpayers to have many addresses or no permanent address.

In the case of my client, she did have the address of one of the children's doctors, but she had a different address for another doctor for a another child. This makes sense, as different doctors will deal with newborns and toddlers versus an older child, but it didn't look great on paper. Then there was the issue of school; the oldest child was attending school at this point, and my client put down a different address for the person in charge of picking him up while she was at work; but again, this wasn't where they lived.

If all of this sounds complicated, it was, and it's why they had three or four different addresses for one of the children, plus the fact they got their mail sent to the home of a different relative. For all these reasons, she couldn't really prove all four of them lived together during the year, which is the only way she could get her credits from the IRS. She provided as much information as possible to the IRS, but it wasn't enough for them to believe they all lived together, nor that they were her children, which is why they denied her claim and why she came to me for help.

The IRS told my client she hadn't proved that she lived with her children, and she couldn't get the refund she was claiming, which was close to $9,000. Just think about that for a minute—$9,000 for this type of taxpayer, someone who makes less than $20,000 a year, is a huge amount. Of course, it makes a difference for everyone; it's not an insignificant amount, but for this young woman, it was half a year of wages, and she wasn't currently making a great income washing dishes—at least not enough to provide care and well-being for her children, so it was a game changer.

Understandably, when she was denied the money, she was very frustrated and upset and called the IRS to try to figure out what went wrong. When she talked to an agent there, he told her he believed her, but that to believe her wasn't enough—she needed to prove it. He suggested she find someone with good experience, someone who represented taxpayers before the IRS. His other advice was to be very careful, because it was going to be her last opportunity to continue fighting for her refund. She came to my office and started having a conversation with one of my associates, who then provided me with the details.

After listening to the whole story and hearing what was going on with her, I decided I was going to fight for her, because I believed we could win. We met, and one of the first things I asked her was if her children lived with her, which for me, is the only thing that mattered to make this case worth fighting for. She told me they did, and at that point, I knew I would take the case. I know from experience that these cases are very time-consuming, but I always take them into consideration because there are people who don't have the means or money for expensive representation.

I told her if everything she was telling me was true, then we would have no problem winning this case. This is something that is very important to me, by the way—I never say *I* will win, I always say *we*, because this sort of work is a team effort. It's not only me who is working, and it's not only for my benefit but for my client. Of course, I needed to ask for various sorts of information and documents, but I needed her cooperation, her trust, and her efforts to do real solid work. In this case, it worked out very well because she provided me with the Notice of Deficiency, which was a big deal; as I mentioned earlier, the Notice of Deficiency is the key to paradise.

With that, we were able to open a case in the US Tax Court, which guaranteed they would hear our case. Before that could happen, though, the IRS required us to provide the documents to support her claims, just as before. And in this case, and many cases with the IRS, creativity is necessary to win. For my part, I asked my client to bring me proof in the form of medical records and school records of her children. At first, she was resistant because those records hadn't worked before, but I told her to ask again and bring them anyway, and so she requested them again.

It's important to note here that when you're fighting for this type of credit, you'll need to use Publications 596 for the EITC and 972 for the CTC, which list the rules for claiming these types of credits. You'll need to meet all the rules to get the credits and money, one of them being, for example, that you live in the same place as your children. Once I had the new documents, I put together a very detailed letter to the IRS. I told them my client was making $18,000 living in Orange County, California, one of the most expensive counties in the states to live in. We also attached affidavits from neighbors and others who knew her, stating that they knew the children lived with her and she was a single mother.

This time around, I told her to get an affidavit or a verification from the person who helped her take care of the children when she was working, confirming that she was the mother. With these new documents, the letter of explanation, and all those affidavits, we put together a package and sent it to the IRS appeals officer. Soon after, I received a call from the officer who said he wanted to have a conversation with me to go over everything I sent in. I explained in even more detail what her situation was, and afterward he said it all made sense, the case was closed, and my client was going to get a refund. Seems almost too simple, but that's how it happened!

I use this example to demonstrate that the best way to win these types of examinations is by providing copious amounts of details, explanations, proof, and of course, by telling the truth. If for any reason you can't prove everything you are claiming, or are in the process of going over the checklist for claiming these credits and end up missing some of the items or even misreading something, it doesn't necessarily mean you won't win— you'll just need to be more creative to provide a good explanation to the IRS as to why you don't have certain documents.

As an aside, I'd also like to offer a bit of advice you might not hear too often, but I think is a good rule of thumb in any situation in which you are dealing with people. As I mentioned, this case with my client took place in 2019 when this type of conference with the office of appeals usually started by telephone, but I remember back in the 1990s, when we dealt with the IRS, these sorts of conferences were almost always in person. Of course, during an unforeseen event—say, a pandemic—it would be impossible to meet in person, but if you can, the added human touch can be quite helpful. Whenever I went to the IRS office with a taxpayer, I always told my client not to send the children to school that day; I suggested they bring them to the interview. Because of where I was located, these meetings usually took place in Laguna Niguel in Orange County, only about ten minutes away from my office.

When we arrived and the appeals officer saw my client's children, one of the first thing they asked the children was who their mom was, and they pointed to her. Now, I'm not saying we won the case simply because of this—remember, we had all our supporting documents and evidence—but doing the interviews in person can sometimes make a big difference as opposed to doing everything by mail, telephone, or fax. It creates more empathy and more connection; a person is more likely to be sympathetic to someone sitting right in front of them.

Something else to keep in mind is this: Due to the amount of fraud committed when it comes to these types of returns, the IRS may also review the tax preparer's files to see how they prepared your taxes. This means people like me take a lot of time and care to make sure the taxpayer meets all the requirements by asking questions regarding every single one of the rules. For example, if a single father comes to me claiming two children, the most obvious questions I'll ask are where the mom is and whether or not he's married. This is important because if he is married, I'll want to know why he is filing his tax return without his spouse, because one of the requirements to claim the EITC is that you can't be married filing separately.

It's important that I, or any professional, ask clients a lot of questions to get to the truth because, unfortunately, sometimes people are trying to game the system and make more money than they should get legally. I prefer to have these interviews face-to-face because it's easier to read subtexts from people's body language and what they are saying or not saying. If the taxpayer starts looking at the ceiling or the floor—anywhere but at me—then it's a pretty good sign they're hiding something.

Sometimes, of course, the interview is over the telephone, and in that case, I must pay close attention to their voice, which is trickier. The IRS always says that the tax preparer needs to make sure they're not getting answers or responses to their questions that are incorrect, inconsistent, or incomplete. If you do receive questionable responses, then you must include that information in your file. My job is telling the truth, so if I think you are lying, I will have to deny my services, even though you are my client. If I don't, then I'll get in trouble as well.

The answers a taxpayer gives need to match up, and the income made must align with the lifestyle, who lives in the house, and everything else that can be taxed, because the IRS will likely take a look in the file. And then, of course, they'll ask whether the taxpayer is entitled to claim those credits. At the time of writing this book (be sure to double-check on the IRS webpage for the current number), the amount the IRS will charge you as a tax preparer, per mistake, is $545 per error. Not $545 per *return*, but $545 per *error*, which as I hope you can see, can add up and cause a lot of financial damage. It isn't worth the risk.

My advice overall is to be very careful in this area. During the last few years I've been representing tax preparers who are facing this type of examination, I've noticed most of them started out by trying to represent themselves. They came to me because it didn't work out in their favor, and the most obvious reason was that if someone works for the IRS, they know their job and have more experience and knowledge than the typical taxpayer. Also, if the IRS is taking the time to select a tax preparer for examination, it's because the IRS already has information that person is committing errors. They will check to see if you have done your due diligence during the interview to better determine if the taxpayer claiming those refunds is legit.

A good rule of thumb when preparing taxes or claiming credits, or anything that may involve the IRS (it's always better to be safe than sorry), is to be proactive, and the way this is done is through questions. As the preparer, I have an obligation to assist you with your tax return and get the maximum refund according to the law, and to do so, sometimes I need to ask private questions. I've had clients get upset or angry, not understanding why I'd need to ask personal questions about lifestyle, for example. What I've learned over the years, and what you need to know whether you're conducting these interviews or being interviewed, is that permission must be granted to ask private and personal questions. As a taxpayer, you can always say no, but if you do, the odds that you get the work done is quite slim. More information is more evidence to help you in preparing and filing a correct tax return to get the best refund possible.

If you answer all the questions, odds are you'll get a better refund, according to the law. In my almost thirty years of experience preparing thousands of tax returns, I've never heard a taxpayer say, "Okay, if that's for my benefit, don't ever ask me those questions." I'd bet for all the years to come, this will remain the case because it's in their best interest. If you're preparing the return, it's also in your best interest because you also want to win. Sometimes, I ask other preparers why they didn't ask all the personal and private questions needed, and they say it was too personal, especially if they'd known their client for many years. And while it may be true, the IRS doesn't know your client. So, you need somehow to ask those questions and document not only the answers but also the questions you asked.

Now, after the interview is done, the IRS is going to look over the file, but they won't contact a taxpayer and conduct an interview to see if he or she qualifies—that's on you as the preparer to set up. They will, however, decide whether they'll penalize you based on the questions you included on the file of your client, either electronically or on paper.

When it comes to the trainings I provide to tax preparers, I always tell them I have good news and bad news (for some reason they always ask for the bad news first). The bad news is that they'll need to know the tax law inside and out to minimize the risk of receiving penalties. I repeat this several times to drive my point home. After that, though, I tell them the good news, which is they don't need to memorize the law. They just need to find a way to get the information, which includes the IRS website and other reputable sources. This, of course, all comes with a caveat, because as I'm sure we all know, our friend Google provides us with a lot of information, but sometimes the information is obsolete. Often, the IRS website is the best place to start and has the most up-to-date information, though it can be quite dense.

My hope is that after reading this chapter, whether you are preparing your own tax return or have hired someone to do so, you feel more in control. I sincerely hope you never get a letter from the IRS to be audited either as a regular taxpayer or tax preparer, and that they never go to your office requesting some files, because if they do so, it means they've found something unsavory. And I'll say one last time, it's my honest belief that hiring a tax expert to represent you is the way to go if you're being audited. It's in your best interest to hire someone with knowledge and experience on this topic to get you out of a tough situation and hopefully save yourself money and stress. At the end of the day, that's what we all want.

CHAPTER SIX

UNDERSTANDING PAYROLL TAXES, LIENS, AND LEVIES

Whether you are an employee or employer, having a deep understanding of employment and payroll tax is one of the smartest things you can do for yourself. In this chapter, we'll focus first on employees, and use some basic numbers to help provide context. Let's say, for example, you make $10 per hour, you get paid every weekend, and you work forty hours a week, which means you're making $400 per week. You might expect to get the full amount in your paycheck, but you don't because of the taxes that get withheld. In this case, the money is being paid at the federal level, which includes income tax, social security, and Medicare.

For the purposes of this chapter, we won't go into numbers on the state level, because it really varies from state to state, but will focus instead on the federal level. Going back to the original example, if you're expecting to receive $400 but you get $350 instead, the question is, what happened to the other $50? That is what we refer to as the payroll tax; as an employee, you need to pay this to the IRS to accumulate money for your retirement or if you need to take an early retirement due to a disability.

An easy way to understand payroll tax is to know it is divided into two parts: the part the employee pays, which we just discussed, and the part the employer pays; they are required to match the Social Security and Medicare percentage the employee pays. This amount is then taken out of your paycheck, and the employer is responsible for sending it to the IRS. The frequency of these payments depends largely on the employer who is required to send them to the IRS on specific dates. These payments could be sent in monthly or semiweekly. The amount held in custody by the employer is known as the trust fund (the amount withheld from the paycheck of the employee).

Perhaps you might be thinking, *But what happens if my employer doesn't send those taxes to the IRS?* It's a good question, and as a matter of fact, I often deal with these sorts of cases. Recently, I was hired by an employer who had a tax liability of several thousand owed to the IRS, because he didn't send them the payroll taxes. He took the money out of the paychecks of his employees, but he didn't send it to the IRS. My first question when I met with the client was to ask why he didn't send this money to the IRS, and his response was he didn't know he had to send the money. I believed him, but this sort of situation really is a nightmare for both employers and employees. If you didn't know you had to send the money in, now you do!

What about if an employer is a business entity, such as an LLC partnership or a corporation? In these cases, many business owners choose to set up a corporation or LLC because they think it will give them protection from the IRS, or that a business entity doesn't have to pay payroll or employment taxes, because they are the owner and not the business itself. Unfortunately, that's not how it works, and the IRS has an administrative process called the trust fund recovery penalty (the trust fund being the money taken out of the employee's paycheck and owed to the IRS).

In this case, whoever owns the business entity is personally responsible for the trust fund, and this is without exception. To use a more concrete example, let's say the trust fund is $10,000. That would mean the business entity is responsible, but also the decision makers of the business are personally liable for the trust fund, but that's not easy to negotiate. What further complicates the situation is the IRS is short on employees (like many other employers), so they have millions of cases to follow up on. The truth is they won't be able to get to all of them, but they will focus a lot more on employment taxes not being paid than other sorts of cases.

The IRS makes it a priority to follow up with those taxpayers who don't pay their employment taxes, and they'll make the assessment with the responsible person or people, whoever the decision-makers are in the business entity. All of this to say, be careful with your payroll and employment taxes, send your payments to the IRS on time, and don't think you won't get in trouble even if you are not preparing the books because, ultimately, you're the one who is in charge and will get fined or penalized if errors are made.

Now that we understand the importance of employment and payroll tax, we're going to go over liens and levies, and the ways in which they can create trouble for you when it comes to taxes. This will depend on when you file your tax return, and whether or not the tax return has a tax liability to pay. If, for example, you file your tax return with a balance to pay, and you do not send said payment, you will get a letter from the IRS, or the Notice of Tax Due and Demand for Payment, which is Notice CP14. This notice is sent to the taxpayer who has a balance due of $5 or more and advises the taxpayer there is a tax due, states the amount including interest and penalties, and requests payment within a specific period of time.

The federal tax lien arises automatically when the IRS sends the first notice demanding payment of the tax debt assessed against you and you fail to pay the amount in full; this is quite serious, as filing a Notice of Federal Tax Lien may affect your ability to obtain credit and employment. Furthermore, a lien secures the government's interest in your property when you do not pay your tax debt, whereas with a levy, the government can take your property to pay the tax debt. If you do not pay or make arrangements to settle your tax debt, the IRS can also place a levy, meaning they can seize and sell any type of real or personal property you own or have an interest in.

At some point, if you don't pay the IRS, they'll start sending nasty letters, warning they'll take all your property, including your assets, your paycheck, your accounts receivable, and everything else you have. If, for some reason, you still ignore these letters, or you do respond but don't have the money to pay, then you'll get a notice from the IRS called a federal tax lien; they'll register the lien in the county in which you live—at that point, your lien becomes public information. Because of this, a lot of clients call me asking why they keep getting phone calls and letters from people soliciting services for tax resolution, and I must tell them because their lien is out there and there are people soliciting their tax resolution services.

If a lien is placed on your property, especially on real estate property, you can't sell the property unless you pay your tax liability. To be more specific, if you wanted to sell your house, you could but any proceeds you'd get, you'd be obligated to use to pay the lien. On top of that, if you have a mortgage, then you'd still have to pay it off. This is a painful process and can be heartbreaking to go through; you'll want to avoid getting into the situation at all costs. There is no way you can stop a lien, though, after you have received the notice, because it means the lien was already raised in the county.

You do, however, have the right to appeal this decision by starting a process called Collection Due Process appeal. What you'll need to do is appeal the decision from the IRS in the time frame provided to you, so make sure you don't miss the date. A lot of people don't realize it's more convenient for the IRS to remove the lien; in certain cases, it might behoove you to do so. For example, I was having a conversation with the IRS once because I was representing a taxpayer who was a financial planner; he was making good money representing clients, and one day a lien was put on him.

This client contacted me and told me he had already received a warning from his broker. He told me if another lien was set by the IRS, he'd lose the appointments he had with various companies he represented, not to mention the millions of assets that he managed. If that all happened, he wouldn't have any income coming in at all. After he told me what his situation was, I spoke with the IRS and told them we'd noticed they had placed another lien on the client. Because of that, he was going to lose his income, which he needed to be able to pay them. So, it was in their best interest to remove the lien because he was making monthly payments. I told them it was better to let my client continue working and making good money and, at the same time, they'd benefit because he'd keep making those monthly payments.

The main difference between a lien and a levy is that a levy can be prevented. The levy can be stopped, unlike the notice of a lien coming after the lien has already been put in place. When you get a notice concerning a levy, it will say something like, "This is your final notice of intent to levy and your right to a hearing." In the same notice, it will state if you don't agree with their decision, you have a right to appeal by starting a process called Collection Due Process appeal, which will begin the process of appeals again.

Another difference is that while the lien secures the government's interest in your property and assets when you don't pay your tax liability, the levy will take the property to pay for the tax debt. If you don't pay what you owe or make the proper arrangements to settle the debt, the IRS will levy and sell any real or personal property you own or you have interest in.

The best way to avoid a lien or a levy is the same, and the simplest advice I can give: File and pay all your taxes in full and on time, and you will be in good standing with the IRS. If you can't file on time or don't have the funds, you need to let them know right away. Don't ignore the letter or think the IRS will go away, as there are payment options to help you settle debt over time. These can be found online at the IRS website, or you can contact a tax professional like myself to help you.

CHAPTER SEVEN

OPTIONS FOR RESOLUTION OF YOUR TAX LIABILITY

Now that we have a clear idea of what to look out for when it comes to employment taxes and payroll, we will move on to some of the more common options for the resolution of a tax debt. Above all else, remember just because you're in debt, it doesn't mean it's over for you. There are still plenty of options, and we'll be going over some of the most common ones here.

FULL PAY INSTALLMENT AGREEMENT (FPIA)

This option, which may be new to you, is a common option taxpayers use to take care of their debts. Before taking this route, though, it's a good idea to understand that the IRS has a set collection period, which is ten years; although you have ten years to pay off your debts, I would strongly advise you not to rely on those ten years. This is because the ten years actually start with the date the assessment is made, but most of the time you won't know the exact date of the assessment. If you have a tax liability or you're a tax professional assisting your client to negotiate his or her tax debt, it's important to find out when the collection period started and when it will expire, aka the Collection Statute Expiration Date (CSED). In my years of experience, I have never seen a period that expires exactly in ten years because sometimes the taxpayer requests a monthly payment plan, files for bankruptcy, requests a Collection Due Process Appeal, or takes some other actions leading to extending the CSED.

Now, let's assume for a moment that the tax liability for an individual is $50,000. The first step would be to complete Form 9465. The maximum time the IRS allows for payment of tax liability is usually 72 months, so you would divide that $50,000 by 72, which is $694.44. In the form, there will be a question of whether you can make the payment, and if you can, you check yes. From there, it's a simple matter of choosing when and how you will send the payment, and then you'll be good to go.

Continuing with this example, if the time left is nine years, then the IRS still has nine years to collect the tax liability from the taxpayer. But what would happen if you can't actually make the $694.44 every month, but you can pay the entire tax liability within the nine years left in the installment agreement? At that point, as long as you are being proactive, you should have a conversation with the IRS to let them know, while you won't be able to pay the same amount every month in 72 months, you can definitely pay it before the expiration date of the collection period, which is another possible option for resolution.

Contrary to popular opinion, the IRS can be somewhat flexible; if you have a good reason, send them the required paperwork and information supporting your claim, and if they believe you'll pay the full amount by the due date of the collection period, they'll work with you. This is not something they state explicitly or go around advertising, though, because it wouldn't be in their best interest. Can you imagine if every time someone called the IRS and told them they couldn't pay their liability or wouldn't meet the deadline, their response was, "Don't worry about it, you just need a couple more years and your tax liability will be gone"? Of course, they're not going tell you that—they'll tell you to pay the tax liability in less than two years because they're working with a Collection Statute Expiration Date (CSED).

The agent from the IRS will always pay attention to the time in which the CSED is approaching, and so will I. As a representative, I need to be in the know, and this is where communication is important between me and my client. Maybe you can't pay the $694.44, for example, but you should be able to make a payment for less than that amount and still pay the entire balance within the nine years left in the collection period.

Once your tax liability is negotiated, the next step is to follow through with your responsibilities, and one of the biggest ones is to pay your installments on time. I let my clients know what to expect if they don't, and it happens more than you might think. For example, I had a client with a tax liability for $111,000, which worked out to a monthly payment of $1,541. I asked him what I ask all my clients—what his expectations were. He was very straightforward with me; he told me he would be able to pay, but just couldn't pay the full amount right now. I asked him how much time he would need, and he said thirty-six months, so I suggested we request even more time, just in case.

From there I contacted the IRS and told them we wanted to set up a payment plan. The employee from the IRS asked how much the client was going to pay, and I said $1,600 per month. They said no problem, and everything was resolved. In this case, my client expressed no issues for paying the tax he owed in thirty-six months, which was the period of time he told me, but we agreed to make it seventy-two months just in case he experienced a cash flow problem in the future. I also told him if he could make payments outside of the agreement to go ahead, which would allow the balance to go down more quickly.

When it comes to making the payments, the process is simple—just go to the IRS website, find the option to make a payment, and make it right there. If you don't want to use their website (and I think this is the better choice), I would highly recommend you choose the option letting the IRS take the money directly out of your bank account. What ends up happening to many clients is they forget to make a payment, or they send it in the mail and it gets lost or delayed. That in turn will create a problem because the IRS is going to think you didn't comply with the requirements, and they can cancel the agreement they have with you. In the end, it's better to provide your bank account information and set up the monthly payments so you don't even have to think about it.

PARTIAL PAY INSTALLMENT AGREEMENT (PPIA)

The next option available to you for resolving your tax debt is called a Partial Pay Installment Agreement (PPIA). This would be the best choice for someone who knows the tax liability is not going to be paid in full by the CSED. Let's assume for a minute that the same client with the $111,000 in tax liability had five years left for their collection period. We would need to divide $111,000 by 60 (12x5) months to get the monthly payment, which comes out to $1,050. After doing this, we would need to conduct a financial analysis, asking questions such as: What is the amount of cash this person takes home at the end of the month? How much income are they generating with their services, and how much are their expenses? Then I ask the client if they can make the payment, in this case, $1,050 per month.

Most of the time, the answer is no, they don't have the money to pay. This doesn't mean all is lost, though, not by a long shot. What it means is now we have to sit down and do another financial analysis, this time one in which we work with the numbers set by the IRS. For example, the IRS provides numbers for housing, so if the client lives in a certain county in a house with four members in the family, the IRS has a set amount they have come up with to spend on housing. To use an example, we'll say the IRS has set the number at $2,000. But what happens if the taxpayer has housing and utility bills for $3,000? That's when we negotiate with the IRS.

These situations can occur in many different areas outside of housing and often is the case when it comes to medical expenses. The IRS provides a specific amount for these expenses, but some people need more money because they have expensive prescriptions or multiple prescriptions, which is not really something they can cut out of their life. This is an instance where we can possibly negotiate with the IRS because the number they allow doesn't apply to their specific situation, and the IRS won't want to interfere with someone's health.

After running a thorough analysis, let's say the client can only end up paying $500; it's not a deal-breaker, but it is something we'd need to prove to the IRS. For instance, we'd send them a copy of bank statements, copies of the receipts they are requesting to verify the client really can't make a payment larger than $500, and anything else they request. After we have proven to them this is the limit of what can reasonably be paid, then it is the client's responsibility to send those monthly payments in a timely and consistent manner.

Recently, I had a client who had a tax liability for $65,000. After the financial analysis we did, she could only pay $60 per month, because we could prove the rest was going to things such as housing, food, clothing, transportation, and other necessary items. Using that amount, if she kept paying the $60 per month, after eight years her total tax payments would be $5,760. In this case, because we were able to prove why she could only pay that amount, the IRS had no other option but to agree. It doesn't mean they weren't going to keep an eye on this taxpayer, and if anything, they would only be more vigilant, but they don't have many options when it comes to these types of cases. Something to add here is my client was a homeowner with a substantial amount of equity. Because of her personal situation, she didn't qualify to refinance and cash out to pay her tax liability.

In this case, the IRS sent a letter stating clearly that they agreed with the $60 monthly payment, but also that they would keep reviewing her financial status in the future, and if something changed—such as she got more income—then they would have to increase her payments as well. But as long as her income didn't change, after those eight years, the IRS didn't have the right to collect money from her anymore. This is another thing they don't love to advertise, but it's the truth, and it's good information to have as a taxpayer. Even when you think your life is over or you're going to go into financial ruin, never panic—this is just another instance proving you always have options, as long as you can show you're in a particular situation where you can only pay a specific amount.

If you are in the process of setting up a PPIA or are in it currently, and if you are a homeowner, the IRS will count that as equity, which is what happened with my recent client. In one of my first conversations with the IRS, they told me she needed to refinance her house and use some of those funds to pay off what she owed. I agreed to talk to her about it, but I knew for a fact she didn't qualify to refinance the house because she didn't hit the required income level. Still, because of my years of experience in the field, I knew that sometimes you need to go through the motions and show the IRS you are serious about working with them and listening to what they tell you. It shows you are capable of following directions and are a responsible person, which they love to see.

I told my client to start the process of refinancing her house; she went to three different mortgage companies and filled out the required forms, submitting the documents they requested. And what happened? Well, she applied and then she got three rejection notices from those mortgage companies saying she didn't qualify. This was good for us, though, because we could use their rejection letters to prove to the IRS she couldn't pay what they wanted her to pay.

I put those applications together, sent them to the IRS, and told them, while it was true she had a house, it was what we refer to as dead equity, because we can't do anything with the equity. At the end of the day, she couldn't get cash out because she wasn't qualified to refinance, and on top of that, the IRS had a lien on her property. If at some point she wanted to sell the property or something changed, and she was qualified to refinance, you can bet the IRS would be there collecting their money because anything she made would go straight to them or toward the debt she owed.

OFFER IN COMPROMISE (OIC)

Sometimes a PPIA isn't the right call for a client so instead we aim for an Offer in Compromise (OIC). In a nutshell, this is a program the IRS has for anyone who owes taxes and is able to qualify. Almost every day I receive a call from someone who tells me they owe the IRS money and they want me to represent them, but what they really want is for me to get the amount they owe the IRS cut down significantly. Unfortunately, it doesn't work that way; otherwise, anyone who owed money and was filing a tax return would be trying to barter with the IRS. It's not as simple as me calling the IRS and offering them a random amount—there are various steps and procedures that must be followed.

Let's assume for a minute that you have a tax liability for $50,000. We already know the IRS has a specific amount of time to collect that money, aka the CSED. If there were seven years left for the IRS to collect your liability, what we would need to do to lower the amount you had left would be to do a complete financial analysis, as with the other options. What is your current income, for example? What are your current business expenses, in the case you have expenses, and what are your current personal expenses the law or the IRS can feasibly allow?

As we know by now, the IRS doesn't allow for all the expenses we claim. They work on what we call "national and local standards." While we can negotiate those numbers to an extent, those numbers are set standards. If we can prove to the IRS in the financial analysis that the total amount the client will be able to pay is $20,000, then the offer will be submitted for this amount, which they will only approve with bank statements, receipts, and other supporting documents. Then, and only then, we can submit an OIC. They'll review it, and most of the time they'll come up with a counteroffer, which the taxpayer either agrees or disagrees with.

The IRS not only takes into consideration the current financial status of the taxpayer, but it may also analyze their background on income generated; for example, maybe the taxpayer has a history of doing well in business but all of a sudden had a bad year; then they will take that into consideration, as well as professional credentials, future income from an inheritance, proceeds from life insurance, business and personal assets, investments, and so on. Most people think this process is quite simple, and almost every day I receive calls from clients asking me to help them reduce the amount of debt they owe. If it were that easy, then anybody could call the IRS and ask them the same question, but it's not—we have to make a very detailed and complex financial analysis, taking into consideration various scenarios to find the best option for my clients.

When I'm representing a taxpayer, I review the counteroffer to see if there is the possibility to appeal the decision and negotiate the amount of the offer down once again. Then, the IRS and I settle the amount the taxpayer owes for a smaller amount. This is where people get confused, because with this sort of case it's not that the IRS reduces what you owe, but rather, they accept the amount you have proven you are able to pay. But in the books, it will still say $50,000 is the amount of the original tax liability.

To give you a more extreme example, I once had clients with a tax liability of over $530,000. This was a husband and wife with no dependents, and when we did the financial analysis, the total amount of the offer we submitted to the IRS was for $300. Usually, the IRS takes about a year to get back to you on whether they agree with the offer, but the law provides the IRS with a maximum of two years to respond. If, after two years, the IRS doesn't give you a response, then it means it's automatically accepted (but the chances are minimal they're not going to be responding within two years, so don't get your hopes up!). While we waited in this case, the IRS was busy requesting paycheck stubs, bank statements, and some other supporting documents during that year.

Eventually we got the counteroffer from the IRS; they stated they didn't accept our offer of $300 and instead proposed $44,000 to settle the tax liability. In this kind of situation, you always have the right to appeal the decision made by the IRS, as we've seen from other examples in this book. After I reviewed the counteroffer, I told my client we had grounds to appeal and negotiated to a much lower amount because I discovered some errors the IRS had made. Still, the client just wanted to settle and thought it was almost too good to be true—he couldn't believe he was going to get rid of $530,000 owed to the IRS for only $44,000.

The client told me he didn't have the money, but would find a way to come up with it by asking friends and relatives for help. He also didn't want to appeal because he thought the IRS would get mad. I tried to tell him they wouldn't, but at the end of the day, he was my client, and he didn't want to take the risk. We closed the case for $44,000—a clear example of how an OIC works. Once again, the IRS didn't reduce the tax liability to $44,000, but in the books it is still listed as the client having owed the original amount of over $530,000.

CURRENTLY NOT COLLECTIBLE (CNC)

We'll move on now to another option for taxpayers with liability known as currently not collectible (CNC). This option brings a lot of benefits; one of them is the taxpayer doesn't have to worry about making monthly payments to the IRS. As we know, there are both local and national standards set by the IRS for how much taxpayers should be spending on housing, food, and other necessities, and the amount can change depending on whether or not the taxpayer is making enough money to cover more than the basic needs. Sometimes a taxpayer doesn't qualify for an OIC because he or she has assets, like a house with equity, and this is what the IRS takes into account—not just the income, but also the assets.

With that in mind, what are the options for a taxpayer who cannot pay beyond their means and has no assets? Despite what some may think, there are ways out, and one of these ways is to request the IRS to place the account into the not-collectible category. The benefit of placing an account in a not-collectible category is that the time that the IRS has to collect the money owed keeps running—remember, this period of time is what we have been referring as the CSED, or until the taxpayer pays what is owed. Let me give you a couple of examples. (As an aside, while the money owed can run indefinitely, it can also be stopped or put on hold, in which case the IRS would stop the levies and stop sending the collection notices to the taxpayer.)

Usually, the IRS reviews the CNC accounts every two years or so, and of course when they do, they will pay close attention to the tax returns, especially if the taxpayer files a tax return with higher income than the income provided at a time of negotiation. If this happens, then the IRS is going to send a notice or make a call to let the taxpayer know they are aware that the taxpayer is making more money. The IRS will then review the case and see if the taxpayer can start making monthly payments. On the other hand, if the taxpayer makes the same or a lesser amount, then it's likely the IRS is not going to do anything.

I remember once a woman came to my office and told me she had a liability with the IRS for over $200,000. I said, "Okay, that's fine, let's review your transcripts with the IRS. During my interview, I asked her how much she was currently making, and she told me she wasn't making any money, but she was receiving some money for being on disability.

My response was most people can't live only on disability; she said she also had a couple of rental houses in Long Beach (an area in Southern California where many of the houses are expensive). When I asked the value of her houses, she told me one was close to a million, which meant she should have $2 million, depending on the mortgage. One of the houses had already been paid off, and the other house had a very low mortgage.

I had to break the news to her that I didn't think we had a case at all, because the IRS was going to ask her to refinance both houses. She was upset because she said she wasn't making any income, and while I agreed with her, I also pointed out that she had two houses. She could sell one and keep renting out the other if she wanted. This was an example of a case where there wasn't much I could do to help her because of the assets she had. And when I called the IRS, I knew they would tell her to sell the house, pay the tax liability, and keep the rest. At the end of the day, it wasn't a great situation for her because she had to pay the full amount, but at least she had a way to clear her liability and keep living comfortably afterwards, which isn't always the case for everyone.

Normally, one of the first things I do when I meet with a client is to review their transcript with the IRS and check the CSED. This specific client's expiration date was in October; she came to me in February, which meant in a few months she would be free of her tax liability. Basically, my conversation with this client was simple. I told her to do nothing, to avoid attracting the IRS's attention. It was up to the IRS to come and seize the assets to collect their money, because in few months, the tax liability would be gone. I set my alerts to run the transcripts after the expiration date shown in the books. I read the transcript and the tax liability was zero, which meant there was no tax liability—another benefit of placing accounts in CNC status.

Another recent client was a man in his late forties who called me one day and told me he had a tax liability for over $200,000 with the IRS. When I asked how he was making his living, he told me he was a truck driver, and in order to have a driver's license to drive those trucks, he needed his US passport. He said he was calling me because his driver's license had expired, and since he couldn't renew it, he had lost his job. I didn't understand why he couldn't renew his license, but he explained that in order to have the type of driver's license required for his job, his US passport had to be active. Because his tax liability was over $50,000, the IRS had contacted the US Department of State to alert them to his situation, so they didn't renew his passport. As a result, he wasn't making any money. When I asked how he was paying his bills, he told me he lived with his girlfriend, who was paying for everything for him.

Overall, it wasn't a great situation because my client didn't have any assets, didn't have any savings, didn't have anything at all. So, we got to work and completed the paperwork, then I contacted the IRS and told them my client wasn't making any money and wouldn't be able to send payments for any amount, that it was impossible given his specific situation. The IRS agreed with us and put his case in a CNC status, followed by a letter making it official.

Once we had the letter, we contacted the US Department of State about his passport. The good news here is there's a provision stating that a passport can be released if the holder's account is placed in a CNC status. A few months later, my client was able to renew his passport and his license. He got his job back and is now working again. Meanwhile the account is still in CNC status. At the time of writing this book, it's been more than a couple of years, and I haven't heard from him, which means he must be doing very well.

INNOCENT SPOUSE RELIEF

Another area that may apply to certain taxpayers is the innocent spouse relief, which applies to a certain group of taxpayers. In this case, you can be relieved of responsibilities for paying taxes penalties and interest if your spouse (or former spouse) improperly reported items, or omitted items, on your tax return. Generally, the tax interest and penalties that qualify for relief can only be collected from your spouse or former spouse; however, if you are jointly or individually responsible for any of the tax interest and penalties that do not qualify for relief, the IRS can collect these amounts from either you or your spouse or former spouse; innocent spouse relief only applies to individual income or self-employment taxes.

Keep in mind here that household employment taxes, individual share responsibility payments, business taxes, and trust fund recovery penalties for employment taxes are not eligible for innocent spouse relief. The IRS will calculate the taxes you are responsible for after you file Form 8857. You are not required to figure out this amount on your own, but you must first meet the specific conditions to qualify for innocent spouse relief, which you can find listed in detail on the IRS website.

Many married taxpayers choose to file a joint tax return because of certain benefits this filing status allows them. When filing jointly, both taxpayers are jointly and severally liable for the tax and any additions to tax, interest, or penalties arising from the joint return, even if they later divorce. Joint and several liability means each taxpayer is legally responsible for the entire liability. Thus, both spouses on a married filing jointly return are generally held responsible for all the tax due, even if one spouse earned all the income or claimed improper deductions or credits. This is also true even if a divorce decree states a former spouse will be responsible for any amounts due on previously filed joint returns. In some cases, however, a spouse can get relief from being jointly and severally liable.

INJURED SPOUSE

Now, let's say you filed a tax return and you're filing as married filing a joint return, which means you and your spouse are filing only one tax return with both of your finances combined, and you have children being claimed on your tax return. This would mean you and your current spouse are filing together, and just to have a number, let's say the tax return you filed qualifies you for a refund of $3,000. To illustrate my point, assume for a moment that your spouse is not current on his responsibility of child support payments. You would get a letter from the IRS stating you had a refund for $3,000, but they sent that money to the state because he had child support he needed to pay. Instead of sending you the refund, the

IRS would send the money to the child support agency; in this case, you may qualify for relief under the IRS's injured spouse program.

If, on the other hand, you weren't liable for child support, then you could complete Form 8379, Injured Spouse Allocation, and send it to the IRS. This would allow you to provide an explanation, such as you understand your spouse had a tax for child support, but it is not actually your issue. Yes, you filed a joint tax return, but individually, you're not responsible for the specific amount of child support not paid. If the IRS accepts your explanation, they will then make some calculations and come up with the percentage of the refund that you're entitled to receive. As this case demonstrates, you were not responsible for the child support, so it wasn't fair for you as an individual in the marriage to lose the money.

Now that we have more knowledge of the various options available to those with tax liability, we will focus more in the next chapter on how to resolve a tax issue with the IRS. We've got lots of tips and resources, including a three-step process to make it comprehensive, manageable, and as stress-free as possible.

CHAPTER EIGHT

OUR SUCCESSFUL STEP-BY-STEP SYSTEM TO RESOLVING YOUR IRS ISSUES

The good news when it comes to having issues with the IRS is that you're not alone. Millions of people in the United States are in some sort of trouble with them, either because they didn't file a tax return, didn't pay their taxes on time, or miscalculated their numbers, among many other scenarios. Not only are you not alone, but by reading this book (including this particular chapter), you will now have more tools and options for coming out ahead, and gaining a whole new understanding of how the system works. Not only will you save money in the future—you may also even make some.

Over the years I've developed a successful system that takes the stress and guesswork out of your tax issues, whether they are minor or major in scope. It also doesn't matter what amount of liability you're dealing with, as I've been representing taxpayers with minimum tax liability, as well as those with a tax liability of over a million dollars. All of that to say, this system is almost universal in terms of who can use it, and it's something applied to every case we handle each year. My system consists of three simple steps, which is how I always divide any activity, task, responsibility, or problem. As one of my mentors, a commercial pilot, told me many years ago, becoming a commercial pilot is very simple—you just need to learn three things: how to take off, how to keep the airplane in the air, and how to land. Since then, I always try to keep it simple.

STEP ONE

The first step we take when working with a taxpayer is to review the account with the IRS to see if the taxpayer is current and up-to-date with their responsibilities, something we like to refer to as "cleaning up the past." And when we review these transcripts and analyze or investigate them, this is when we'll be able to see all of the good things as well as the bad things. To be honest, most of the time when we review a transcript, it's already a mess because the client has come to us because they have a tax liability. So when you come to us, this is why we begin by reviewing your case and making sure you are current with your responsibilities as a taxpayer, such as having filed all past returns you are responsible for.

When you have a tax liability, most of the time it's what is known as a civil case problem, so nothing happens per se—you just pay your money and you'll be squared away, or if you do not have the money to pay, you can negotiate your tax liability. However, it's not always that simple since we know when people don't file a tax return, it may turn into (if it hasn't already) a criminal case because not filing a tax return is a violation of federal tax law. As you know by now, the IRS pays very close attention to people who don't file tax returns, so it's important we make sure you are current with your filing responsibilities, including tax returns, but also anything else like payroll tax returns or any other kind of reporting responsibilities.

After this, I have a conversation with you to go over my discoveries. We will also review the period the IRS set to collect the money, which is the CSED. Then we go over some questions regarding your past, current, and future financial position in order to give a better recommendation of the options you have to resolve any back taxes. There is also the review of the payments. Suppose you have made several payments but you find the tax liability goes up instead of down. How can that happen? The payments you send are applied to your account, but sometimes the interest is higher than the payment itself. This is why it's critical we use our system to review in great detail the transcripts of the account in order to provide you with accurate information regarding payments and the status of the account.

Something we always do is call the IRS and put the collections actions on hold; in the conversation, I'll let them know you are aware you are not in compliance with making estimated tax payments or by filing tax returns, but you know what you need to do now.

Conversations and open communication are a big factor in success when it comes to dealing with the IRS, which is why I always ask my potential clients if they're willing to follow my recommendations, because if they don't, then I won't be able to resolve their case. I'm not sure why, but sometimes the taxpayer thinks that by hiring me, I will solve all of their issues, but it's not true. What we do is actually teamwork, and it's vital for my client to provide me with information and supporting documents in order to put together the case. I'm very clear about this from the start, and I tell them I need their commitment to cooperate with me to resolve the issue(s). If they agree, and after reviewing everything and cleaning up the past, then I call the IRS and put a collection on hold for their account.

Once I represent a client, we start getting to work immediately. When I talk to the agent from the IRS, I always tell them I don't take cases where the taxpayer doesn't make a commitment to work with me in earnest, which is something the IRS likes to hear. They want to believe that some accounts will be taken off the books or out of the collections. On top of that, it's also very costly for the IRS to have an account in collection because it involves time, resources, sending the collection notices to the taxpayer, and sometimes the collection agents—Revenue Officers—are the ones in charge to collect the money. Not only is it a costly system, but it's also a lot of work, and if they can have less to worry about, they'll be happy.

Again, they like to hear the taxpayer is going to be in compliance and is working with me, and most of the time they'll agree to work with me. They pull up the account, review the transcript of my client, and are willing to provide me with all the information I need. Of course, I need to have the correct power of attorney to show I'm entitled to receive the information for my client from the IRS, and I'll also need to list all the items for the client I am representing.

Before we get to into the negotiations section, I want to be clear that the IRS won't be willing to talk to me about payroll tax, because payroll tax is not specifically listed in the power of attorney. Outside of that, though, once I have all the information from the IRS, I'll know what the next steps will be for my client. Step one is nothing more than an investigation and review of the transcripts of your account with the IRS to find out the total tax liability and reporting responsibilities that have not been met.

STEP TWO

The second step is where we provide you with recommendations to follow, which may include filing prior tax returns for previous years, because the IRS won't even listen to your case if you are not all caught up on your returns. Therefore, it is one of the most important actions to take in order to get in compliance when it comes to filing prior tax returns. When that is settled, we can give you recommendations, such as when you should start making the estimated tax payments for the current year so when the year ends, you will already have paid the balance for this year and the tax liability will not be increased.

During this step we'll also discuss how to avoid making the same errors or taking the same actions which could lead you to having more tax issues in the future. For example, sometimes when the payroll tax is an issue, we tell the client they need to be current with their tax deposits. Most of the time the taxpayer's behavior must be modified. It's their behavior which led to their tax problems in the first place, so it's important to correct these actions in order to avoid the same patterns later on.

It may seem incredible, but sometimes when I interview clients, I ask them what returns they owe to the IRS; sometimes it's one or two, but sometimes they are missing several years. When I find that out, nothing else can happen until the issues are cleaned up right away. Otherwise, when we call the IRS to negotiate or put a stop on the collection, they'll tell us right away the taxpayer hasn't made any estimated tax payments or is behind with their reporting responsibilities. Of course, before that happens, as I said before, I have a very straightforward conversation with my client about what it means for me to represent them. It means the IRS will stop contacting the taxpayer, and I become responsible for the actions of the taxpayer, so it would behoove them to comply with the law.

Sometimes one conversation is enough to drive the point home, but sometimes it takes several. The point is the client needs to behave themselves, otherwise I'll withdraw my power of attorney. And that's it—they'll be on their own without my protection. Most of the time they agree, and if someone doesn't, then it's an easy decision to part ways before we get too deep in a case. Once in a while, when I analyze a case and see it may become a criminal case, I choose not to represent them— not because I don't want to help them, but because if I represent someone who has done something illegal, then I'll also end up becoming the best witness for the IRS and their worst enemy.

Why is that? By law, if your case becomes criminal and if the IRS asks me for information about what you told me or documents you gave me, then I'll have to provide all the information to them. I'd inadvertently become the best witness against you for the IRS, and it would be very difficult for you to win. An alternative to this situation, however, is if it does turn out to be a criminal case, you can hire an attorney, and then if the attorney needs to, they can hire me to work for him. The goal of step two is to be current with all your responsibilities as a taxpayer.

STEP THREE

Once you are in compliance, we can negotiate your tax liability with the best option and move into step three, which is straightforward because we already did the most painful and tedious part of the process. Step three is still very important, but it is a lot simpler because all the hard work has already been completed—all that's left is to gather and collect new information as proof. Then, we'll need to complete the paperwork required to prove to the IRS our case was the appropriate option. In this stage, we need to be very creative without violating the law, and what we do in this phase is the main reason you hire us.

At this stage, I'll have another conversation with you, letting you know after the cleaning, analysis, and thinking about protecting your best interests, this is the best deal I can offer according to the law. If you agree, then we submit the paperwork to the IRS and start the negotiation process. As you know from the prior chapter, the IRS provides fixed numbers of the national and local standards, so they will take some time analyzing that against what we provide.

All of this is a negotiation because sometimes the IRS needs more information than what is provided on those standards; for example, when it comes to housing and utilities, sometimes the standard amount makes sense, but during some months the client may have had the air conditioning on all day and all night long because it was summer and over 100 degrees. Or maybe in the winter, they had to run the heater in the same way as the air conditioner, twenty-four hours a day, which means the electricity bill is going to fluctuate.

If the utility bill is higher than what is provided by the standards from the IRS, we can negotiate and tell them you need more than the standards. As always, we'll need to provide supporting documents in order to substantiate our claim. Another area is food, which has a standard amount for a family. But special circumstances happen. For example, perhaps you have a doctor's recommendation to be on a specific diet with specific kinds of foods, and the cost for the special foods will be higher than what they have set as a standard. We'll always argue for your health, which also brings to mind cases in which a taxpayer doesn't have health insurance. We recommend to taxpayers that they buy health insurance, because health insurance is an expense acceptable to the IRS, as is a reasonable payment for life insurance. You may even have the right to buy a new car to replace an old car.

When we plan and negotiate, it's not only with the IRS, but also with the taxpayer, in order to minimize the amount paid, but also to protect the taxpayer by giving recommendations to the IRS they're more likely to accept. As shown in the previous examples, there are a wide variety of options we can take in order to minimize the monthly payments or to minimize the amount of the offer we are going to negotiate with the IRS, including placing the account in a not collectible status.

To reiterate, the three steps start with reviewing a taxpayer's file, cleaning it up, then having a conversation with the taxpayer regarding the expenses allowed by the IRS and, most of the time, doing some planning to reduce the payment we will propose to the IRS as a resolution of the tax liability. It may seem simple and straightforward on paper; sometimes, I do have people call me and ask why they should hire me if they can just do these steps on their own. While I would never tell someone not to try, the truth is the IRS won't provide you with anything outside of the straightforward information of the national and local standards and whatever is online. The IRS exists to protect government interests, not to protect your interests. That's why most of the time, when you hire someone to represent you, not only will you have a better chance of getting a better deal, but you may also even save some time and money.

Additionally, all the expenses for representation are deductible and, most of the time, will reduce the amount of the payment or offer proposed to the IRS for resolution. Say, for example, after completing the financial analysis, the offer we propose to the IRS is $7,000, and the fee to represent you is $3,000; we can then reduce the amount of the offer from $7,000 to $4,000 because the $3,000 you'd pay for representation is an allowable expense—in other words, you won't pay my fees, the IRS will. On the other hand, if we went with a monthly payment plan, and after the financial analysis the amount was $300, you'd make a payment for representation for $100, and the payment to the IRS would be for only $200, instead of $300. A question for you, therefore, is whether or not you or the IRS will pay my fee—the answer being the IRS.

CHAPTER NINE

YOUR RESPONSIBILITIES AFTER RESOLUTION OF YOUR TAX LIABILITY

If you've reached this point in the book, take a moment to congratulate yourself—we're almost at the end of our tax journey. I'm so glad you trusted in me, and in yourself, to widen your knowledge and options when it comes to dealing with finances, taxes, and the IRS. In this chapter, we will focus on the resolution of your tax liability, the most common conditions that occur, the "probation" period of an OIC, how to stay in compliance, and more.

Once you and the IRS reach a deal, they'll lay out some conditions and responsibilities for you to follow and stick to in order to keep the terms of the deal. I colloquially define the probation period, which is not the term the IRS uses, as the five years after the offer in compromise is accepted. For our purposes, it makes the most sense for our discussion.

Some of those conditions are straightforward and nothing out of the ordinary, but are simple responsibilities you must keep up with to be in compliance with the IRS. For instance, you must file your tax returns before the due date, including extensions. Another responsibility to keep in mind is when you file your tax return, there should be no outstanding tax liability. What that means is that if you are a business owner, you should have been making those estimated tax payments throughout the year, according to your income. If you are an employee, you should have a correct withholding from your paycheck—this last recommendation is not mandatory, but it helps. Otherwise, when filing your tax return, if you did not have a correct withholding, most likely your tax bill will be high, which can put you in a situation where you are not able to pay it. For the OIC, if it was accepted as a lump sum, then the payments must be made on time and periodically when they are due. It's a simple matter of paying attention to the dates and making sure you're on the ball with what you owe; if you set up automatic payments instead of signing onto the IRS website every time, you won't even have to think about it.

This responsibility should come as no surprise, as it is the most basic element, and staying in compliance for taxpayers is nonnegotiable. The IRS will be clear about informing you this is now your responsibility, and if you can handle it, they won't bother you. Another thing to note here is the IRS will not increase the tax liability you owe; they'll stay at the specific amount was set for you, whether it is income tax, payroll tax, or other kinds of taxes, which should put many people's minds at ease. Still, the IRS may revoke the prior agreement for not complying with your responsibilities. In another words, basically they want you to be the "perfect" taxpayer.

In terms of time, in the case of an OIC, the period of probation will be a period of five years; however, what happens if the resolution wasn't through an OIC and instead was a payment plan? In that case, the IRS will enforce the responsibilities made at the time of the agreement. If you don't meet the requirements, don't file your tax return before the due date including extensions, or don't make the payroll deposits on time, it will be pretty cut and dried: The IRS is going to revoke whatever the negotiation was if it wasn't an OIC, and you will get a letter saying you failed to comply with your responsibilities.

This sort of situation is especially sad because the taxpayer went through all the effort and work to come to an agreement with the IRS, only to fail to comply with the responsibilities and lose it all. The only way to salvage this situation, potentially, is to be proactive and notify the IRS as soon as possible in order to avoid any misunderstanding on their side. If I were representing a client in this situation, I would call the IRS right away and explain the situation to let them know the client was not in compliance, but we are fixing it now and it won't happen again. In short, it is important to follow the recommendations and instructions stated in the letter from the IRS.

Despite the simplicity of the rules—follow the conditions and don't be late—people don't always do what they need to while on probation. If you don't follow the conditions, the IRS will revoke the agreements and the negotiation without hesitation, because it's in the best interest of the IRS to get money from you and not wait. And remember, this applies not only for income tax but also employment taxes, payroll taxes, and other reporting and obligations of individuals and businesses.

CHAPTER TEN

TO MY COLLEAGUES

I'd like to take some time here to address my colleagues. While I hope we all succeed individually, I also want to make a case for working together, especially if a former or current client contacts you for an audit representation, audit examinations, or tax returns you prepared for them. My first question to you would be, would you represent your own client, even though it may be a conflict of interest? I would advise you to think seriously about this before entering a contract, as the examiner of the case will ask if you have the knowledge and experience to represent clients. And while it may be tempting to say yes or to have a bit of overconfidence in your skills, I believe the risks outweigh the possible benefits.

For example, the examiner in charge of the case may look at the tax return and say that they noticed the taxpayer you're representing claimed 20,000 miles driven, so they need proof of the mileage by looking at the mileage log. If you don't have the proof or documentation, they'll come back and ask why you included it in the tax return in the first place. At this point, you might get flustered and tell them the numbers you have are the numbers your client gave you, but the examiner won't accept that. As the representative of the client, it's your responsibility to get the facts, so it will be seen as your fault for not asking more questions and getting proof and the necessary documentation.

Now, if you find yourself in this unfortunate situation in the future, I can bet you'll regret ever agreeing to do an audit representation. It's a lot of work, time, and investigation, and my best advice is to really think about this the next time a client comes to you for an audit representation of a tax return you prepared. Not only may it be a real conflict of interest, but it will also probably be more work than it's worth. Another word to the wise is if you have said yes, or are thinking about saying yes, to representing a client in an audit, don't be fooled by the examiner or the IRS agent. They may be polite, nice, and helpful, but at the end of the day, if the IRS decides to audit a tax return, it's because they already know something is amiss. They aren't going to be spending time on cases or files with a ton of information, documents, and proof; they're going to look at what's not adding up, where there are errors—and for you and your client, it'll be an uphill battle.

From my experience, I know that one of the keys to success when it comes to audit representation is to play the game with the rules provided. We forget sometimes the rules set by the IRS are made to protect the government's interests, and not the taxpayer's, and they will do what they need to do to get the money owed to them. This is why being knowledgeable and having a good strategy is critical to come out ahead, and once you have it, there are a few things we can do as tax professionals for the benefit of the taxpayer.

As someone who has a lot of experience in this area and knows how to play the game, I would highly advise my colleagues to contact me so we can work together. Before that, though, you'll want to ask as many questions as possible of your client to know what their situation is. Once you have a good idea, then I would suggest having the taxpayer contact me so we can work together on this. I've been doing this for many years and, as a matter of fact, a major source of prospects in my business come from other tax professionals and accountants nationwide.

I'll say here, too, if you are going to represent a client in an audit, then you'll need to know the law backward and forward. If you don't think you have the proper knowledge and experience, we have nearly thirty years of experience representing clients and are happy to help. When tax preparers reach out to me in these situations, I always assure the preparer that the client is theirs; I'll concentrate only on representation and not on other services such as tax preparation, payroll, and bookkeeping. I'll never go against you or make you look bad—sometimes clients come to me and blame whatever mistakes there are on their tax preparer, but I always correct them. I remind them it wasn't the tax preparer's fault—it was theirs—because at the end of the day, they're the one who provided the information to the preparer, and most of the time the client doesn't even review the tax return.

If they are defensive, they might claim they didn't review the return because they don't know how to prepare tax returns, and while that may be true, they do know (or should know) the numbers, especially if they're a business owner. Most of the time the taxpayer is the one who is responsible for the mess, though they don't always want to admit it at first. If you refer a client of yours, I'm committed to working together, and because of that, it's a good opportunity for all parties involved. If we work together, you will have the opportunity to make more money by providing other services because, most of the time, when a client comes in for an examination, they usually also need additional services like bookkeeping, and you'd be the one to do it. I'm very clear with the client—and this is also mentioned in my engagement letter for services—in the event the client needs additional work, such as cleaning up the books, preparing documents, and completing questionnaires with information on payroll, it will be an extra fee, and I'd recommend the client hire you for those services.

If we decide to work together, then you'd need to provide the necessary information to me, such as the financial information, income, assets, bank accounts, and retirement accounts. We know what happens with a lot of the taxpayers—our clients start completing the paperwork, they write their name in, sometimes they write the address, and then, suddenly, they're tired. They stop completing the forms because they see it's too much information and very time-consuming. Most of them are not used to the amount of paperwork, so you're going to have the opportunity to assist them and make some additional money.

Another thing to keep in mind is that a high percentage of taxpayers who have a tax liability with the IRS stop filing returns because they think if they do file a tax return, the IRS will know they exist and where they live. For some reason, they believe that by not filing tax returns, their problems will go away. But, of course, we know the problem will not go away; it will only get worse. This means a lot of times clients will need to file tax returns for prior years, which is what you'll do if we work together. When they hire me, I can represent them for an audit or to negotiate a tax liability they may have.

You can also advertise you provide tax resolution services if you have the knowledge and the experience, and then do what I did before becoming an Enrolled Agent—I assisted my first client back in 1996 to help them out in tax court. I wasn't representing him, technically, but he came with a bunch of papers and asked for help because he didn't know what to do. I started reading what he'd brought me and told him he had a right to request a petition with the US Tax Court.

I gave him a list of places he could go in order to get representation, but he didn't want to; he insisted he only wanted my help. Since I wasn't representing him, and I wasn't an attorney, I couldn't give him legal advice, but there was nothing wrong about helping him fill out the paperwork. Sometimes, when I had to call the IRS, and they said I didn't have the authority to call on behalf of a taxpayer because I wasn't a CPA, Enrolled Agent, or an attorney, I simply said I wasn't representing him, but he's right here, and he wants to give his authorization for me to explain what he doesn't understand. Of course, not everything can be done this way and at some point, you will need to be in communication with the IRS; otherwise, you may end up hurting the taxpayer more than benefiting them.

If you don't have these skills, we'll be happy to provide tax resolution services, and at the end of the day, it's imperative you advertise your services as much as possible. As I mentioned at the start of this chapter, I truly want all my colleagues to win, and I know there is more than enough business to go around for what we do. It's in all our best interests to share clients and to work in the areas in which we feel most adept and capable.

FINAL THOUGHTS

I'd like to remind everyone reading this book that everyone in the United States will, at some point, become a taxpayer because we all make our living by receiving income. And according to the law, everything is taxable, unless it's specifically excluded by the law, and by now we all know the rules are constantly being modified and updated. But, in a nutshell, everything we receive—and I'm not talking just about money—could be considered a benefit, income, asset, or gift, and as I said before, everything we receive is taxable unless excluded by law. I believe this is a country that embraces people and wants to help them succeed, but there are also laws and regulations to follow, just like in every other country.

At the end of the day, life will be less stressful, and you'll sleep a lot better at night, if you get your finances and taxes in order—that goes for all taxpayers, including myself. And if we can make some money by hiring the best person to help us with our taxes, why wouldn't we? Whoever you think has the knowledge and skills to minimize your tax liability without breaking the law is someone to invest in because you'll also be investing in yourself and your future. That is an option in life we all deserve.

ACKNOWLEDGMENTS

First of all, I want to thank God for the opportunity he has given me to serve others. To my beautiful wife, Silvia, for always supporting me and for always being there when I need you the most—I love you with all my heart. To my beautiful daughters, Kary, for all your teaching about personal growth, and Laury, for your commitment and hard work; and of course, to my lovely grandson, Sebastian. To my brother, Carlos, and my sisters Lulu, Lupe, Coco, and Tina, we had options and found a way to go through when we lost our father. To all the members of our team, The NAVA Group, for believing in my dream.

And last but not least, to my mentors who have shared their wisdom with me—you know who you are—especially to Michael Rozbruch, who taught me the "secrets" to running a very successful tax resolution business.

ABOUT THE AUTHOR

MR. NAVA holds the highest recognition with the Internal Revenue Service (IRS) as an Enrolled Agent. He is able to protect, represent, and defend taxpayers before the IRS with their income tax problems in all fifty states. He has been in the industry since 1993, holding ample experience in the field. Mr. Nava is a trainer, speaker, and mentor to tax professionals nationwide. He is also the founder of The NAVA Group Co., LLC, which specializes in providing business owners accounting, tax planning, tax preparation, payroll, insurance, and advisory services. Their headquarters are located in Irvine, California; however, they serve clients nationwide.

FIND OUT MORE AT THENAVAGROUPCO.COM.